THEY ALL WANT MAGIC

NUMBER SIXTEEN
Rio Grande/Río Bravo
Borderlands
Culture and Traditions

Norma E. Cantú
General Editor

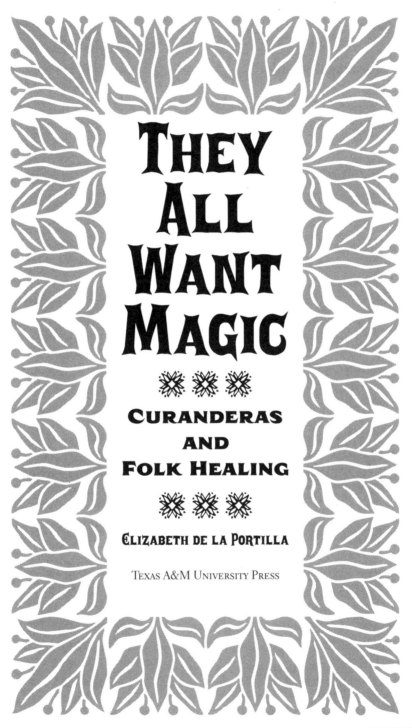

THEY ALL WANT MAGIC

CURANDERAS AND FOLK HEALING

ELIZABETH DE LA PORTILLA

Texas A&M University Press

The paper used in this publication meets the requirements of
ANSI/NISO Z39.48-1992 (Permanence of Paper).
Binding materials have been chosen for durability.

Library of Congress Cataloging-in-Publication Data
Portilla, Elizabeth de la.
They all want magic : curanderas and folk healing /
Elizabeth de la Portilla. — 1st ed.
p. cm. — (Rio Grande/Río Bravo ; no. 16)
Includes bibliographical references and index.
ISBN-13: 978-1-60344-099-8 (cloth : alk. paper)
ISBN-10: 1-60344-099-2 (cloth : alk. paper)
ISBN-13: 978-1-60344-114-8 (pbk. : alk. paper)
ISBN-10: 1-60344-114-X (pbk. : alk. paper)
1. Hispanic American women healers — Texas — San Antonio. 2. Medical
anthropology — Mexican-American Border Region. 3. Healing — Mexican-
American Border Region — Religious aspects. 4. Herbs — Therapeutic use.
5. Biculturalism — Mexican-American Border Region. 6. Mexican-American
Border Region — Civilization. I. Title. II. Title: Curanderas and folk healing.
III. Series.
GN296.5.U6P67 2008
306.4'610972'1 — dc22
2008034983

Dedicación

Keta, Jaime, Donna, Elizabeth Claire, Edward
Thomas, and Emily Victoria (the little dragon)

TABLE OF CONTENTS

CONTENTS

ACKNOWLEDGMENTS

BLESSINGS. That is how I see my life: full of blessings. They take shape in the many people who have supported my efforts and counseled, pushed, and prodded me along during this long journey. The healers who spoke with me and became my teachers were infinitely patient with my questions. Lizzie Brieno, Jo Ann Ramos, Jacinto and Fela Madrigal, and Charlene Beacham deserve my many thanks. Esperanza Ytuarte gave me a historical viewpoint of San Antonio I had not considered. There were elements of the spiritual practice of *curanderismo* that were explained in great detail to me by Berta Valdes. Thank you, Mrs. V.

Throughout the process of rewriting and revisions, Mary Lenn Dixon at Texas A&M University Press never wavered in her support. Mary Lenn's encouragement helped me get through the doubts I had initially about combining my storytelling with the academic text. Norma Cantú's advice, guidance, and astute reading of my text helped clarify salient points. She seems to know what I am thinking better than I do at times.

As I often tell my students, none of us get to where we are without standing on someone's shoulders. The academic shoulders I have leaned on and looked over are spread out across the country. Ruth Behar, Richard I. Ford, Antoñia Castañeda, and Eliseo Torres are people whose knowledge and training I value a great deal. At the University of Texas at San Antonio, Dan Gelo, Betty Merchant, and Robert Milk supported and encouraged me at every turn. I would be remiss if I did not acknowledge two women in San Antonio whose creative voice and activism inspired me to think about the arts as healing: Barbara Renaud Gonzalez and Sandra Cisneros.

Special thanks to Andrea Brennan and Thom Lemmons for their careful reading of my text and their thoughtful insights.

I'm grateful for the support that my friends Sharon Navarro, Felecia Briscoe, Cecilia Sandoval, Elizabeth Enciso, Lucila Ek, and Johnny Lyon were always ready to give me. And, my family, thank you for all the stories.

The table of plants and the healers Aida, Virgilio, and Maggie were part of my early work in curanderismo while I was at the University of Texas at San Antonio, which resulted in a journal article, "Comanche and Mexican-American Curers: A Regional Approach to Folk Medicine," in *Touchstone*, published by the Texas State Historical Association.

"So what is it
that people want
when they
come to see you?"
I asked.

"They all want magic.
La cosa es — the thing is —
there is no magic,"
Golondrina answered.

INTRODUCTION

IT IS SPRING OR EARLY SUMMER during my childhood in Corpus Christi. Our backyard is covered in cilantro (coriander). Tall, green, feathery plants sway in the breeze, their white flower heads so compact that bees walk across their petals with complete confidence. Towards dusk my mom sends me to gather the leaves that season our evening meals; the smell of tortillas and simmering beans follows me out the door. I enjoy walking through the weedy herb patch, my feet crushing plants here and there, sending their aromatic oils into the evening air. If I hold a flower head very still, a bee will land. Lost in its own harvest, it will amble onto my thumb or forefinger without awareness. There is no fear of getting stung, having learned early on that the key to observing nature is in being still.

When a coriander plant blooms, its leaves change. They go from a flat, toothy, cloverleaf shape to a thread-like greenery resembling dill. The energy of the plant goes from leaf production to flower growth. As a child the logic of this does not occur to me. All I know is that the broader leaves taste better and are prettier; those are the ones for which I search. Flat, dark green leaves are the ones that will go into our *olla* of beans and chile.

In my mother's scattered garden are other herbs she uses not only just for food but also for minor illnesses. There is *estafiate* (*Artemisia ludoviciana* Nutt.) for stomach aches, *boraja* (*Borago officinalis* L.) for fever, and orange tree leaves for calming teas. Peaches, pomegranates, and chile plants are sporadically raided for their fruit. The *solar* of my girlhood is not large. Ten lots of equal size line our side of the street and another ten across from us make up our block. But every household is predictable in its array of vegetation. There are a variety of flowering plants in the front and side yards. Lilies, roses, gardenias, and hibiscus are the most popular. Sometimes there is a large tree or two, palm or chinaberry, or maybe a fruit tree of some kind. Mesquites or orange trees are for the backyard. Herbs and/or vegetables grow in every yard.

This is a poor working-class neighborhood where many people are one or two generations removed from a *campesino* background. Our agrarian roots make themselves visible. Chickens sleep in mesquite trees; roosters crow in the morning. Rabbits are raised for food, and corn grows above the chain link fences delineating each neighbor's yard. The women in the neighborhood heal their families with simple cures using whatever is at hand. Nothing is written down, things are just "known." I grow up knowing that a warm garlic clove wrapped in cotton and placed in my ear would cure an earache in the same way I know the sun will rise the next morning.

This was my world, all I knew. I'd know nothing different until I was eighteen years old and away from home for the first time. At university in Wisconsin, I learned that not everyone had an existence like mine. People did not regularly gather their own herbs or grow their own fruit. The idea of using something green from your yard to cure a stomach ache was unknown to many of my friends. It was as unfathomable to them as their lack of knowledge was to me. Nor did they leave their homes to harvest fields of cotton, strawberries, or beets, as many of our neighbors did, as had my parents. Still, we had learned the same history in school, spoke the same language, watched the same television shows, and read the same books. How could we be so different?

It was the first time I felt as if I did not belong and yet was not totally on the outside. I could not share these experiences from home with my new friends; we did not have a common cultural language. It went beyond class and economics; it was a difference in how we understood the world.

Such is the case now. Through my academic life, I seek to make the experiences of those I work with part of the everyday fabric of the greater American culture. I want "outsiders" to understand that a worldview that is different from the common majority is not out of place in the everyday. It is not a new theory. It is one that until recent history was not readily discussed or applied within our own borders.

As a native anthropologist I have the benefit of memory as a starting point for my work. It was invaluable when interpreting data, formulating interview questions, and establishing relationships. As a native ethnographer the benefit is in not just knowing general information about the area, the people, or the topic but in easily understanding the nuances of culture, remembering how to address an older person, and knowing to use the formal *usted* instead of *tú* when first approaching people older than myself. It is letting an elder dictate the rhythm and length of an interview, when it starts, and when it ends, because being quiet and holding one's tongue is as important as knowing when to speak.

The outsider's perspective added to the knowledge gained through my academic studies. I can see theory in practice on a personal as well as professional level. I work in neighborhoods and with people very much like those of my girlhood, people from the same economic and social class. I have learned that the concerns of one generation are much like those of the next. The working-class subjects participating in my study are of my generation. If I had not had the benefit of an education, my life would fit very neatly into theirs. They are friends and family; they are not a distant foreign folk who can be left in the field for the comfort of a veranda or the solitude of a tent. My immersion in the field has been total — psychologically, physically, and emotionally. In truth, I carry it with me always and cannot imagine a day that does not begin or end without an anthropological observation.

The tension between insider/outsider positioning can be precarious. Linda T. Smith, Director of the International Research Institute for Maori and Indigenous Studies at the University of Auckland, New Zealand explains that as an insider you are sometimes held to a different standard than an outside researcher; questions are asked of you in some fashion that are not of an outsider. Questions such as "Whose research is it? Who owns it? Whose interest does it serve?"[1] These questions are not overt but are part of our conversations when we first enter the field and are developing relationships. I was asked: "Who is your family?" "Where did you grow up?" "When did your people cross (the U.S.-Mexico border)?" "Why are you doing this work?" Part of what people are asking is, "How long after you finish will you remember us?"

Nonnative anthropologists can make the claim that, given time, anyone can reach this level of immersion in the field. But how much time? It is one thing to *learn* a culture; it is another to *be* a culture. In this lies the crux of my dilemma. Am I so close to the culture that I miss opportunities for investigation? Will I be fair in my assessments?

The nature of my work and positioning add the issue of subjectivity to this text. This is not a work of distance but one of constant "making," of revisiting sites of knowledge production, identity construction, and the changing culture of the borderlands. It is a work that leans heavily on the concepts, writings, and the lives of anthropologists and non-anthropologists alike; those who are not part of the dominant class, marginalized because of ethnicity or gender — the "halfies" whom feminist Lila Abu-Loghod wrote about, and halfies one step more in that they are marginalized within their own communities because of their academic lives and their rise on the socioeconomic ladder. These factors separate those like my colleagues and me from our students, our families, our backgrounds, and our target populations. Arguably, other immigrant waves have experienced this in American history. There is always that first generation that leaves the enclave as it moves into the middle class and beyond.

But for many of us entering academia and the middle class, leaving also means a return. Not satisfied with personal gains, my colleagues and I feel an obligation to get involved. Whether this means serving on a community board of some kind, organizing, mentoring students, making other community service efforts, or pressing for more minority hires, activism is a part of who we are, on university grounds and off. Many of us are the realization of the Chicano movement of the 1960s and 1970s, but there are too few of us. In this post-Chicano age, the number of scholar activists is small relative to the population. We are of multiple worlds: working class, poor, middle class, elite, white, brown, boundary crossers, observers, teachers, and subjects. We emerge as another thing altogether in reflection of a people who occupy multiple spaces at the same time, the borderlander.

I first heard the term post-Chicano used by an artist local to San Antonio. Cruz Ortiz, twenty-six, well educated, with a wife and children, has a reputation as a cutting-edge artist. He and I have talked about the changing face of activism since the 1960s. For Cruz it is history; for me it is part of my life. However, we both agree that the cultural coalescing exercises of *El Movimiento* that brought us to this point need to reflect current times. We have to work in the present. This means not a separation of cultures but a creation of something else altogether.

Cruz often takes folkloric and iconic elements known to many Latinas and Latinos and weaves them into social and political critiques. His paintings use the self-deprecating humor noted by Américo Paredes, John O. West, and others who are part of the Southwest Texas/Northern Mexico character.[2] His work and that of others in this area are indicative of a people who are aware of their differences/sameness with the world around them and that an intercultural dialogue is in place on different levels.

Anthropologists are taught that the people with whom relationships will most likely form while in the field are marginalized beings, "native" intellectuals who are ideal subjects in some ways because they are often insightful about their communities and are eager to talk with someone they see as a mirror of themselves. But as a native anthropologist among others like me, I am that marginalized being both in the field and outside of it.

Invariably, when I tell people I work with curanderas, they will say, "I was cured with an egg once. My_____ [insert mother, aunt, grandmother] rubbed an egg all over me and then broke it into a glass of water, and put it under my bed."

"How did you feel when it was all over?"

"Oh, okay, better. But I don't believe in that stuff."

Egg stories, they are my favorite. They bring back memories of girlhood and warm embraces, when a smooth, cool, elliptical object and a grandmother's prayers could cure the worst things in life.

This is not just my girlhood but that of many generations of Mexicans and Mexican Americans. This book is about the touching on of these stories, of memories retrieved, and of voices that are distant but never truly silent. This is a mix of memory, anthropology, cultural activism, and our search to make ourselves whole. My objective is to present curanderismo through an anthropological lens and also present how I see its underpinnings in community activism through the arts, social justice, new healing modalities, and in mending the deep wounds of historical transgressions. We are all healers and just need to be reminded of it.

CHAPTER 1

❋ ❋ ❋

The Road Home

What is so great about Texas?
The vastness. It is the depth and
breadth of the place. When I
drive through Texas, it is an emotional experience every time.
The landscape changes subtly
but markedly; mile after mile it
is never boring. Texas has distinct geographical areas. In the
northern area, the Panhandle is

flat prairie. Dust devils swirl all about, kicked up by combines, tractors, and the wind. The Native Americans of the area believe that witches live in the dust devils and will paralyze you if you are not careful. Far West Texas has canyons, desert, and mountains. South Texas is fertile, humid, and hot. East Texas is green, piney, and swampy.

Home is more than eight hours away once I cross the Texas-Arkansas border. I spend the night in Longview on the eastern side of the state, just a few hours away from Louisiana. This is still the South. The speech of the people here has a distinct drawl (think Lady Bird Johnson). The Bible Belt runs solidly through here; fundamentalist religions — Southern Baptists, Church of God, Pentecostals — keep their hold on the population. It is a conservative area, morally and politically. Some counties are still dry; you cannot buy liquor within their boundaries. My ex-husband, Johnny, was born and raised in this area; he got into trouble once as a teenager for calling an African American, "sir." My mother-in-law told him, "Don't ever let your father hear you call a black man 'sir.'" I never sleep well in East Texas.

The next morning brings the last leg of my journey. Driving into Central Texas, the pines thin out, live oaks and cedars take over, and the land starts to roll. Hay fields dot the landscape, as does cotton and sorghum. Cactus makes an appearance, clumping up along fence lines, its purple fruit well protected with arsenals of thorns.

Driving through the state, I recall the history I learned as a child and compare it to the history I learned as an adult. As a child, I learned of the white pioneers making their way into the wilderness, fighting Indians and coyotes in order to tame the West. I learned that Texans fought for independence from a corrupt and uncivilized country (Mexico). I pass historical markers telling of battles won and lost during the Texas Revolution. Later I learned the other history, of East Texas and its history of slavery, where white and black children learn early on the hierarchy of power that sets order. Towns like Jasper are a part of this landscape. Jasper is where a black man named Byrd, chained and hitched to the back of a truck, was dragged to death and in the process decapitated by young white men. I wonder whether his last moments were filled with the sharp smell of pine resin so heavy in the morning air or the sound of his flesh being scraped off by the asphalt road. I was told once that our sense of hearing and smell are the last to go in dying, and I can only imagine what it was like for him as his heart came to a stop.

In West Texas, the history is of eradicating the native population, closing off the land by wire and railroad, and cutting people off from territories long occupied. In the South, it is of segregation and exploitation of the Mexicano. I have read accounts of Tejanos[1] in this area, men, women, and children lynched in groups by riverbanks. Letter writers describe the smell of their rotting corpses lingering for days. All of this is the past and the present; it is part of the land and I drive through it with ghosts for company.

I catch the road to Austin. This is the Edwards Plateau, a limestone shelf cut out of the earth eons ago, rich with flint and rivers. San Antonio is ninety miles beyond the capital, south and west on the edge of a place called the Balcones Escarpment. Here the hilly limestone meets the central coastal plains. It is an ecologically rich land, which depends largely on an underground water source for its survival. In some high places you can see for miles, and the sunsets are in hues of lavender and pink.

In my life before academia, I owned five acres with Johnny on the edge of the Hill Country, just north of San Antonio. The sunsets were our favorite times. Against the pastel colors of the evening, we often saw turkey hens gathering their young. We listened to the first calls of the whip-poor-wills, their melancholy cries echoing back and forth. The wind can come in fast and cold in the winter, and you can see the boughs of the Live Oaks give way to currents of air; waves of cold nip at your face as they rush down the side of the hills. In the spring, the flowering of milkweed plants announce the imminent arrival of Monarch butterflies, plant and insect having developed a symbiotic relationship through the ages. In a good year, the evening sky is dotted with their fluttering shadows as they land in our oak trees to overnight.

By contrast, forty miles away, in the low spots on the south end of the city, banana trees, palms, and papayas grow. You would swear you were on some wayward coast of Mexico. Life can bloom several weeks early on this side of town in the spring. The wildlife, even in the most urban of areas, varies from common sparrows to red-tail hawks. In a park near my present home, I have seen a family of ring-tail cats (*Bassaricus astutus*) sunning along the upper ridges of a limestone outcrop. I have noticed wild varieties of *estafiate* and *gobernadora* (*Larrea tridentate* (DC) Coville), which I thought were only found along the border area.

There is a sense of belonging for me, of being part of the land, of knowing that I am in the fabric of the place. History is written on the faces of people. The colonizer and the colonized meet in the features of those who pass you on the street, who wait on you at a table, or who give you directions at a street corner. Code switching is the lingua franca. It is not Creole Spanish but more of a soupy mess in which everyone partakes: Mexicanos, Mexican Americans, African Americans, and Euro-Americans alike.

Frankly, anyone who makes this area home cannot escape it. Businesses that are ever opportunistic in their quest to enlarge their market share make use of this phenomenon. You can order a *papa con* egg taco and not get a quizzical look. This is home.

San Antonio

In San Antonio, a regional culture exists, largely reflecting the influences of two nations: The United States and Mexico. Unlike many large U.S. cities, it is not a place comprised of a single dominant power structure with different ethnic enclaves. San Antonio is largely a bilingual, bicultural city: this is reflected in its economic and cultural life. It is a city in cultural negotiation, and I believe this reflects the changes many U.S. cities are undergoing or will be experiencing as we move towards a more intercultural society.

According to the U.S. Census, San Antonio is the seventh largest city in the United States, and its socioeconomic enclaves are fragmented by a freeway network that crisscrosses the city. It is a gateway to the borderlands region because of its proximity to the *frontera* (150 miles) and because the infrastructure of the city facilitates the movement of goods and individuals to and from the border area.

The larger metropolitan cities — Houston, Dallas, and San Antonio — are connected to each other by wide highways and then dissected every which way by the roads leading in and out of town. When in San Antonio I find myself driving wherever I go. Nothing is within walking distance, and getting to and from places is commonly described in terms of "drive time." This constant driving allows me to think about how the layout of the city reflects the differences in the racial and socioeconomic backgrounds of its citizens.

Physical structures in the urban landscape of a city can be anticipatory indicators of how people think of those outside their immediate neighborhoods, of one another, and of themselves. As well, they are markers of boundaries and designators of one aspect of social identity.

The first of these asphalt boundaries is two highway loops that surround San Antonio. Loop 1604 circles the outskirts, and Loop 410 lies within the city. The roads leading to other places — IH 35, 37, 10, and 90 — crisscross the city east, west, north, and south. These four roads converge in the downtown area, further dividing the inner parts of the city by forming a small ring around the tourist-rich hotels, restaurants, and businesses that are the economic and political heart of the city. All the roads together make up the skeleton of the city on which commerce is built.

Those living north, west, and outside of 1604 are usually well-to-do and Euro-American. There are Tejanos who are upwardly mobile or those whose families came as early settlers. There are very few African American families in this area. This area is the start of what is called the Texas Hill Country originally settled by German immigrants. Mexicanos say that the Germans took the prettiest land but the most unproductive. You cannot grow a thing out there — it is all limestone and cedar. However, the views are fantastic. Houses are built to fit the landscape: stone, oak, and cedar buildings. Some are renovated farmhouses, and others are new modern homes built on two or three-acre lots in subdivisions with names such as Walnut Creek or Oak Knoll. The subdivisions are often constructed with many restrictions as to how the lots can be used. This serves to ensure that families of a particular income level will live there as well as those who hold like-minded attitudes about how the area should be developed.

The residents living west and south of 1604 are Mexican, Tejano, or Euro-American and some are small-acreage farmers. The landscape is flat and sandy but productive. Corn, watermelon, peanuts, strawberries, and sorghum grow in this area. The roads in this direction lead to Corpus Christi, Laredo, and the border. The average income is much lower than in the areas previously described. The homes here vary tremendously. There are a few subdivisions, but they are not nearly as restrictive as in the Texas Hill Country area. Many homes in this area are old homesteads; there are newer brick buildings built by people who have moved from the city. Also, you will get more multi-family homes built on lots: two houses or a mobile home for extended family members.

Southeast of the Loop are commercial enterprises, the railroad, and Houston. Northeast is the corridor connecting San Antonio and Austin with outlet malls between the two; it is an area of continuous commercial growth. Most African Americans live on the city's east side, though there is movement towards the marginal areas around the city's center. On the northeast side is a small but visible Asian presence, both newly arrived immigrants and those long settled; this population is largely Korean and Vietnamese.

As you come in to the city from Loop 1604 from any direction, the composition of the neighborhoods pretty much reflects what is outside. Income decreases as you get closer to Loop 410, but the ethnic makeup stays much the same. It is not until you get inside Loop 410 that things change. The

Loop (as it is known) is about four to six miles within 1604 and about eight miles from downtown. Inside the Loop, incomes fall quite a bit, as a general rule. The neighborhoods are largely Mexican American. The exception is northeast San Antonio. Here live long-time residents, the middle class, and Euro-Americans, though they have seen property values level off as growth moves northwest. There are also small enclaves of well-to-do families in central San Antonio whose homes are among the oldest in the city.

Physical structures, like highways and railroads, divide people socially and economically as much as they serve to divide a city geographically. This holds true for San Antonio. The oldest families living in the city are usually north of central downtown. The new families who live within the Loop are usually immigrants from Mexico, in neighborhoods south and west of downtown. Locals believe it is better to live outside 410 and in the northern part of the city. This is reflected in real estate values and services available. A small, one-bedroom apartment in north San Antonio will rent for over $700 a month; a small, two-bedroom house in an area where one healer resides costs about the same in monthly rent.

The encircling of downtown San Antonio by the converging highways provides a barrier for the tourists, who are the economic blood of the city, against the poverty that lies just outside the ring of asphalt on every side. It is ironic that immediately on each side of downtown live the poorest and worst educated of the city, yet the center of town generates a great deal of civic wealth.

There is a restaurant in the middle of El Mercado, in the city's center, named Mi Tierra, which means "my land." It is open twenty four hours a day, and both locals and tourists frequent this San Antonio dining institution. When Denise Chavez was in town promoting her book, *Loving Pedro Infante*, several of us took her to Mi Tierra for dinner after her talk. Around the table sat women writers, columnists, a local activist, and an artist who enthralled us with stories of her recent visit to Kuwait. Apparently, male Kuwaitis did not know what to make of her — this strong, vivacious, independent woman. At the table next to us sat a young couple with a new baby. I felt comfortable and in good company. Tourists, recognizable by their very fair skin, cameras, and whiny children, sat all around us. *Trios* and *mariachis* milled about the tables offering their five-dollar songs. The men — the musicians are always men — are a fixture at the restaurant. They have peddled their songs here for as long as I can remember.

We sat and laughed for a couple of hours. I listened to stories of writing and family and of their adventures. People constantly made their way in and out of the restaurant — Mi Tierra is quite a popular spot. We flirted with the waiter and drank margaritas. This place has always seemed more like a place of ritual than just a restaurant. People from all walks of life come to eat here. High or low in economic standing, they all find their way to this restaurant. For the tourists it is a requisite stop; for the locals it is the Mexican Denny's. At our table sat three of the country's best known Chicana writers, yet in San Antonio, a city that prides itself as the home of an emerging Mexican American intelligentsia, they sat unrecognized. The same happened to Linda Rondstadt when she came to Mi Tierra — that is, until she started singing with the floating *musicos.*

The basement of the restaurant, where the sweet bread is baked, once served as a meeting place for the city's local Mexican gamblers. This is a small piece of history that few people know. My father was a bagman in his youth for one of the gamblers. My dad was a handsome man, a *pachuco,* when he was young. He lived for trouble and apparently San Antonio was the kind of city that could give plenty. It has that air of ill repute in some quarters. This section of the city center, where the tourist market place is now located, was once the Mexican side of town. There were well known social borders dividing the downtown area between the Anglo and Mexican populations; the whites had the Alamo and Mi Tierra was the equivalent of a capital for the Mexicanos.

The restaurant is the anchor for Market Square past and present. Here, it is Christmas 365 days a year. Colorful ornaments and lights hang from the ceiling. As you enter, the bakery is the first thing you see, and like the eatery, it never closes. As a child, my parents often brought the family here to eat and we would walk around the *mercado* afterwards. Then, it was a real market, which sold produce and dairy as well as clay pots, piñatas, and Mexican goods. My favorite childhood place was the open-air section of the market across from Mi Tierra, where produce was sold. Flat bed trucks brought seasonal vegetables and fruits, along with spices and herbs. The concrete floor was often damp from the ice that kept the produce cool and light bulbs hung haphazardly from the rafters, illuminating the entire place. There was always a great hustle and bustle going on with Mexican *ranchera* music playing in the background, old timey music beloved by my grandparent's generation. The songs carried in their lyrics tales of hot times along the border, battles, love, and struggle.

Vendors sold to families and businesses alike. They called out to prospective customers who walked by, proclaiming the quality of their goods and the freshness of their fruit. Melons so fresh they had slept in the field the night before, mangos fresh off the trees in Mexico, and avocados ripe and ready. The ice, used to keep things ripe, also served to cool the place down a bit. The atmosphere was always carnival-like but at the same time earnest. Produce that did not sell meant lost revenue when it spoiled. Until the late 1980s, produce and spices were still available in one section of the mercado, after that it changed to the kitschy tourist area it is today. All that remains of the old market is a reminder in the form of a renovated farm truck, parked just inside the entrance of the produce market with bushel baskets full of papier mâché vegetables and fruit on its flatbed. The artificial produce on display is eerily ultra real in its brilliant color and fake imperfections. On either side of the truck are silk and crepe flowers, beautiful — but dead.

The transformation of this area in downtown San Antonio from a working class space to a tourist haven is based in commerce, not social reform. I primarily know San Antonio through family history and, until I took up permanent residency in the late 1980s, as a tourist destination. My birthplace is Corpus Christi, on the Gulf Coast of Texas. My father's family has deep roots in the San Antonio area, and it is because of his family, primarily uncles and aunts, that we spent many of our summers in this town. One uncle, Tio Jesse, was the caretaker of the McNay Art Museum. He worked for *Señora* McNay before she died. She bequeathed her mansion, a large Spanish-style building, and an art collection to a foundation; my uncle continued to live on the grounds in a small cabana. A parking lot now covers the spot where his house was. Every summer, for many years, my parents brought us to San Antonio, and we stayed with my uncle in his small home. We were not allowed into the mansion, by then the art museum, during the day, but we had the run of the grounds, which spread around the house in a circular fashion. There was a pond filled with minnows and koi. We would tease crawfish out of the tiny streamlets that branched off the pond. The vegetation was green, lush, and fragrant, with beds of flowering plants everywhere.

At night, fireflies lit up the small lawn in front of my Tio's *casita*. It was at this time of the day when we made the journey up to the house. The shrill sound of *chicharas* (cicadas), calling to one another in the oleanders, quieted as we walked past the lamplit stairway leading to the front door. The house is built around an open patio, Spanish style; doors leading through this open space give the visitor the impression of walking into a tropical hiding place. A large raised tiled pond sits in the open center.

I remember chasing my younger brother and sister through the museum, sliding on the polished wooden floors, none of us realizing that the tapestries we hid behind were icons of European art. We used to go around the rooms together trying to pronounce the artists names; Vincent we understood, but—Van Gogh? We were warned not to touch the paintings, but what child can resist the allure of bright colors and raised brushed strokes? If they were within arm's reach, we touched them.

In reflection, it was a surreal time. For a few weeks every summer we left our *barrio*, with its *cantinas* on every corner, and lived on the grounds of an art museum. My parents would take us to the zoo and to the other museums in town, as well as to the mercado. Economically, it was inexpensive — museums at that time cost very little or nothing to enter—and my parents were social creatures; they enjoyed being out in public spaces. What I have learned of late is that we frequented that area of downtown because of social boundaries. While places like the Alamo and the Riverwalk were open to us because we were tourists, there were parts of downtown San Antonio to which we had no access. The McNay was an exception because my uncle had the key.

Esperanza Ytuarte grew up in San Antonio. She is in her mid-forties and is a police officer. In the course of her life, she has journeyed from a poverty-level existence on the Westside of San Antonio to a comfortable middle-class environment. We spent an evening with two other friends exploring downtown San Antonio. I kept wondering why we stayed so close to the area around the mercado. We never walked past St. Mary's Street that runs east to west and where city buses travel towards the southern and western parts of town.

The Riverwalk, the Alamo, big hotels, upscale retail stores and Hemisphere plaza are between Soledad and Highway 37, which is the border between downtown and African American neighborhoods. Esperanza explained that as a child she was not allowed to go past Soledad, which is one street up from St. Mary's. Esperanza explained, "I used to sell candy and fruit as a kid. The shop owners left us alone pretty much. There were a lot of us who made money this way; we all knew each other. We looked out for each other. We knew we weren't supposed to go past Soledad. From Soledad to Frio was Hispanic. That other side was for Anglos."

When I pressed her to explain how she knew, there was not anything she could point to that told me this was a codified rule; rather, it was segregation by social prohibition. Joske's, a local department store comparable to Macys, did not allow Mexicans in their building until after the 1950s. It was a fixture of upscale traffic in San Antonio's downtown area and was less than a block away from the Alamo.

As we wandered through the downtown area, I learned that Mexicanos frequented particular theaters—the Aztec, Alameda, and Nacional; whites went to the Majestic. White retailers had stores on the Mexican side of town — these were places like Woolworth's or Penner's, where things could be bought on layaway. We quickly realized that the railroad leading to the stockyards, the Mercado, the Cathedral and the jail were all on the Mexican side of town. This area between Frio Street and Soledad is the oldest section of San Antonio as a municipality, but at some point it became working class and almost exclusively brown. The center of this outward growth was the Cathedral and Military Plaza. Richard Flores writes, "Due in part to the railroad and the emergence of capitalism after 1875, San Antonio underwent a deep spatial restructuring whereby the commercial center shifted from Main and Military Plazas to the area around the Alamo. This relocation had important social and spatial consequences: it marked the transition of San Antonio from a Spanish-Mexican town to an American city."[2]

The shift eventually developed into a social stratification of racial groups that continued actively until the 1960s. Esperanza's experience as a child vendor began in the 1950s and continued into her adolescence. By that time, active segregation was no longer practiced in the commercial areas, but the effects of it are still visible. The lower-end retail stores are still between Soledad and Frio Streets. University Hospital, which serves the poor and indigent, is in that part of town. There are fewer bus stops as you near the Alamo, so the workers of the big hotels on the Riverwalk or near Alamo Plaza, who rely on public transportation, have to disembark between the street boundaries described by Esperanza.

We ended our walk through downtown with a visit to the Riverwalk; I had not been there in years. A friend had told us of a tile marker with the scene of a Mexican in a tree shooting at white Texans by the river. We found the marker. It sits at the bottom of the stairway that leads up to St. Mary's Street — the boundary Esperanza could not cross as a child. The plaque tells the legend of the cypress tree which stands beside it. The legend states that the tree was frequented by snipers (Mexicans) who shot at the Texans (Anglos) when they came to the river. Legend or not, the marker is a physical manifestation of the deep divide between the two groups and how that divide is made active in public space. Sometimes we do not have to look to history or legend to see how the city continues to mark its citizens.

On July 29, 2000, two young girls were murdered:
   A dark, filthy, and long alley runs behind a Westside corner bar with gray walls full of graffiti. This is the same alley, leading to the neighborhood library, where the bodies of two fourteen-year-old cousins were found earlier this summer. It was in this alley behind the

bar where the teens became victims of an attempted sexual assault shortly before their deaths, according to a court document made public Saturday. The document, called an arrest affidavit, reveals some of the alleged details of the teens' final hours. The document alleges that two men were seen attempting to sexually assault the two girls in the alley behind the Commander's Bar in the 1800 block of Buena Vista. One of the girls momentarily escaped her attackers as her cousin was being pinned down, the document states. Then the girls were choked, thrown in a trunk, and dumped behind the Bazan Branch Library.[3]

Many on San Antonio's Westside were angry and shocked at the death of the girls. The church community and others offered a reward for information on the killers. The area where this crime occurred is close to the city center, it is just out of the downtown area, not too far away from El Mercado.

What struck me was that on the night the girls were being murdered, police officials deployed a large number of officers to the downtown area to patrol the city streets against teenage drivers. The reason given: Tourists needed to feel safe in their visits to San Antonio. Inner-city teenagers have long made Saturday night cruising night. They converge on the downtown area to visit, show off, and generally behave as many teenagers do across the country. Less than five minutes away, possibly as the girls were dying, police were driving down empty but safe streets.

In the days that followed, I neither saw nor heard anything in the media that posited these two events next to each other. But for me the message seems clear. The tourists are worth saving, but a poor Latina is not. The city, in this manner, marks its citizens and encodes them with a particular status that is understood by anyone who lives here.

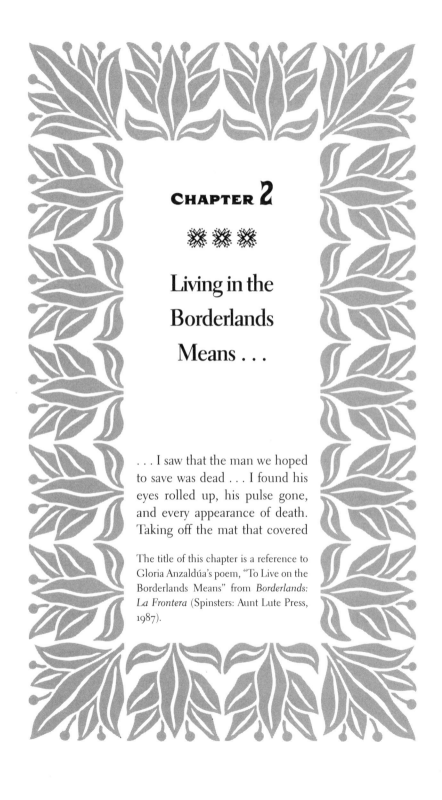

CHAPTER 2

❋ ❋ ❋

Living in the Borderlands Means . . .

. . . I saw that the man we hoped to save was dead . . . I found his eyes rolled up, his pulse gone, and every appearance of death. Taking off the mat that covered

The title of this chapter is a reference to Gloria Anzaldúa's poem, "To Live on the Borderlands Means" from *Borderlands: La Frontera* (Spinsters: Aunt Lute Press, 1987).

him, I supplicated our Lord on his behalf and on behalf of the rest who ailed, as fervently as I could. After my blessing and breathing on him many times, they brought me his bow and a basket of pounded prickly pears [as payment]. . . . When we got back that evening, they brought the tidings that the "dead" man I had treated had got up whole and walked; he had eaten and talked [with those there]. . . .[1]

Eliseo Torres, who wrote *Green Medicine*, argues that Alvar Núñez Cabeza de Vaca was a curandero (perhaps the first) because of his blending of indigenous cultural material with European religious ideology in order to function as a healer during his travels through the Spanish borderlands. Torres wrote a position paper comparing the methods of Cabeza de Vaca with three well-known healers of the border region: Teresita, Don Pedrito Jaramillo, and Niño Fidencio. He concluded that:

> In summary, Cabeza de Vaca could be considered the first curandero or shaman from the old world who healed in the Southwest. This conclusion is based on a comparison of Cabeza de Vaca's healing experience with those of three of the most famous Hispanic curanderos who influenced Mexico and the Southwest. All three traditional folk healers lived in and had followers throughout Northern Mexico. The commonalities of the three curanderos and Cabeza de Vaca were that they all were considered folk saints, or saints of the people, while they were alive; they all used rituals in healing the sick; they all believed that religion and faith played an important role in their healing; they all were charismatic leaders; all believed that they had a gift, or don, from God to heal; they all possessed extraordinary powers and performed miracles.[2]

All of this does fit into general descriptions of curandera/os, but the most interesting thing about Cabeza de Vaca's life is not mentioned by Torres: his transformation from conquistador to curandero. What Cabeza de Vaca experienced was life-changing in the same manner that the healers I work with have reported, where one's identity is changed into something else altogether.

Alvar Núñez Cabeza de Vaca came from an aristocratic Spanish family known for their battlefield exploits and for being part of the different *conquista* movements that pushed Spanish boundaries beyond their European borders. He came to the Americas as part of the Narvaez expedition for "God, King . . . and money." The expedition was ill-fated. After wrecking off the coast of Florida and wandering through the Southwest over a span of nine years, he and an ever-dwindling number of survivors made their way to Spanish settlements in Mexico's interior. Along the way Cabeza de Vaca, in turn, was a slave, a healer, and a trader. His life among indigenous people changed him profoundly. He became a marginalized person; he learned what it was like not to be the one in the majority, the one with power or hegemonic rule. He survived this by adapting and negotiating a new identity. This brought not only a chance of survival, but also a change in his status from one of exclusion to one of community inclusion and prestige. He became a bordercrosser.

Much is written on the border experience and how its residents are shaped by the circuitous flow of commerce and culture.[3] Robert Alvarez, in his review of borderlands literature, argues that the borderlands are iconic and can be used as a paradigm to understand, among other things, power relations between the Third World and the First.[4]

The power relations that define people in San Antonio have their antecedents in the conquest of the New World by the Europeans. The rules governing attitudes and conduct among the population mirror the precepts set upon native people by those who colonized the territories of the Americas.

The history of the U.S.-Mexico borderland area is one of conflict at different levels. Since the arrival of the Spanish, then the French, and finally the Euro-Americans, the borderlands region has been an arena of political, social, and economic conflicts. Sometimes those conflicts have been bloody encounters, culminating with the extermination of certain groups of indigenous people. Language and cultural groups have disappeared into the dominant group through genocide, disease, or assimilation. That is not to say that conflict did not exist before the arrival of Europeans. The archaeological record can attest to various encounters, violent and otherwise, among the different groups of the Southwest. Nevertheless, the setting of boundaries, conceptual and real, by the technologically superior Europeans hastened the demise of many groups in a fashion unseen in previous times. These boundaries were geographical in one sense, dividing territory amongst themselves (Spanish, French, American, and then Mexican) but there were also social and class boundaries.

Among the Spanish there was a socioeconomic hierarchy that stratified people according to 1) status and 2) blood quantum. Native people occupied the bottom rung, *mestizos* a step above, then *gente de razón* (people of reason, those of European descent whose families included no Indian or African blood) at the top. Gente de razón were holders of political power and economic well being, while native people at the bottom were the worst off, politically and economically.[5] They were on the margins of society and had no voice in government. For a time early in the Spanish conquest, they were held as slaves. The practice continued for decades.

Native people were considered barbaric and savage. It was believed that they should submit to the will of the Spanish as "matter yields to form, body to soul . . . animals to human beings . . . the imperfect to the more perfect, the worse to the better."[6] It was not until Friar de las Casas argued on their behalf in front of the Council of Valladolid in the mid-1500s that they were granted status as people. Even so, it was in a marginalized, paternalistic fashion. "[The Indians] will embrace the teaching of the gospel, as I will know, for they are not stupid or barbarous but have a native sincerity and are simple, moderate, and meek. . . . For they are docile and clever, and in their diligence and gifts of nature, they excel most people of the known world."[7]

Friar de la Casas was sincere in his quest to change the attitudes and treatment of those who came under Spanish dominance, but his language conveys the underlying sentiments that he sees the Indian as a creature of the wild. By using phrases such as "native sincerity" and "gifts of nature," there is nothing to indicate in his language or writings that native people were thought to have any intellectual sophistication equal to that of Europeans. This manner of thinking is a harbinger of the noble savage idea touted by Rousseau and set the tone for European attitudes towards indigenous populations, as well as validating in America treatment and exploitation of its native people. Therefore, it is not surprising that in the reporting of historical events by various sources there is often a reflection of prejudices born from years of social and political stratification.

David Montejano is an historian who explores relations between white settlers of Texas and Mexicans in the period of 1836 to the mid-1900s. He is interested in conflict but reports it using the writings from newspapers, official documents, and correspondence, as well as archival material to let those voices speak to the present. It is a powerful presentation.

Conflict, as Montejano's writings show, occurs in an everyday sort of way. Bolton, and those like him, speak of history in what Montejano calls "triumphalist literature." Montejano uses the mundane to show conflict at work. For example, he provides a passage from a journal by Mary Jaques, an English woman on a visit to a Central Texas ranch in the 1880s. In it she writes that it was difficult to convince Texans that Mexicans were human. "The Mexican seems to be the Texan's natural enemy; he is treated like a dog, or perhaps, not so well."[8] This was written nearly fifty years after the Texas revolution. However, sentiments by the majority of Anglo Texans, who were in political and economic power, ran against anyone who was Mexican or of Mexican descent.

However, conflict is not just violent encounters. We can understand conflict as an everyday contest between people or groups of people who have cultural, political, social, economic, and language differences. It is like wearing two pieces of fabric against one another. In spots, the fabric is worn thin; in others, there is hardly any wear at all; and yet sometimes the fabrics cling together. These stories present different kinds of conflict in action. Moreover, I believe they are representative of many common experiences of men and women along the border.

Scope of the Project

San Antonio's Westside neighborhoods are largely working-class Mexican and Mexican American. Here, the tradition of folk healing, curanderismo, is very visible. What I propose to show is that the philosophy of traditional healing, as practiced in the Texas borderland area, does two things: one, it allows the healer to reconstruct his/her life through the experience of having a healing gift revealed in a spiritual fashion; because of this, two, he/she is able to assist others in transforming their own lives. These two points give curanderismo its efficacy.

Curandera/os draw people into the web of culture as they heal and at the same time create bridges between cultures. For the communities they live in, they are cultural brokers, helping their clients to construct a whole out of fragmented worlds in which they can function. Using ritual, symbolic, and plant material, they assist their clients in constructing a social and cultural identity that helps them better their lives.

The value in understanding this type of healing philosophy has a practical application. By understanding how traditional medicine systems work in a large, urban setting, better use can be made of social agencies and public health facilities.

I serve on an advisory board for an organization at the medical school in San Antonio, The Center for Integrative Medicine. The board is a panel of individuals from various segments of the medical academic community. Our goal is to educate the medical community on ways that alternative methods can aid in the traditional practice of medicine. My presence serves as a sign that curanderismo is seen as a viable healthcare option in this area.

Beyond this application is the more abstract understanding of how groups with power, the political and economic majority, and groups that traditionally are disenfranchised from institutionalized power structures negotiate for space and coexistence. San Antonio is such a place. The practice of curanderismo is prevalent in areas that historically have exhibited a great deal of social dynamism but that remain politically and economically marginalized. Curanderismo is not the driving force in the quest for social, political, and economic change that marks San Antonio's South and Westside. It is a strategy that its inhabitants use in dealing with factors that seem out of their control — the loss of a job, legal problems, government agencies, the threat of deportation, and the threat to cultural and self-identification.

I make use of theories in identity construction, medical anthropology, and ethnobotany in my research. The issue of subjectivity is discussed in chapter three; the fourth chapter is a discussion of the history of curanderismo and its structure; the fifth and sixth chapters discuss its presence in San Antonio as practiced by my consultants; and the seventh chapter contemplates the future of curanderismo. The healers operate from different *niveles* or realms that constitute the tradition. A discussion of the *niveles* is taken up in chapter four. Healers will access elements from the different niveles to enact a cure.

I have interviewed twenty curanderas and curanderos as well as some of their clients during my research. At times I practice what I call grab-and-snatch ethnography, collecting data whenever and wherever possible. The people I work with do not make a full-time living as healers. That is not possible. My time with them collecting and processing information varied from half an hour to a day trip on the border. Rarely do I go two weeks without talking to consultants like Golondrina or Jacinto. If I do not call them, they call me. In this fashion, we amble on.

By reviewing the established work in curanderismo, certain areas stood out for me as under-researched, including gender, life experience, and identity construction. In large part, it is my belief that this tradition is largely framed as a health care system in an applied fashion and not as an institution that reflects culture and its construction. Also, work in medical anthropology is an emergent subfield of anthropology. Therefore, there has been a certain lag time in the application of these areas to curanderismo.

It is also a case of academic bias. Because curanderismo is something that occurs in a local (meaning U.S.) population, it is not "exotic;" and exotic is what often draws the attention of anthropologists. As well, there seems to be a disregard in anthropology for the work that minority scholars undertake in other academic fields. While in anthropology seminars and classes we may read essays or works by historians, literary figures, or social scientists from other countries, we do not engage the work by Mexican American scholars and writers like Robert Alvarez or Gloria Anzaldúa.

Using borderland theory and medical anthropology with the writings and theories of those in the area of community activism and feminism, I believe I can offer a new perspective of how traditional medicine systems like curanderismo work and why they continue to flourish. Some of the early work done in documenting curanderismo had a sense of salvage ethnography, as if its demise was imminent (because of the acculturation process) or that it was a primitive system that was out of date and "quaint."[9] In my fieldwork there was no evidence of the demise of curanderismo.

Curanderas and curanderos readily engage the world around them. Because of this it is important to approach the practice in the same fashion that Emily Martin approaches her study of the immune system and our notions of health: "My intent in juxtaposing the present and the recent past is to 'defamiliarize present practices and categories, to make them seem less self-evident and necessary' (Sawicki 1991: 101), to describe at least some of the 'connections, encounters, supports, blockages, plays of forces, strategies and so on which at a given moment establish what subsequently counts as being self-evident, universal and necessary' (Foucault 1991: 76)."[10]

This quote speaks to the heart of the study of curanderismo. The work now has to go beyond what is comfortable and familiar. There are elements of curanderismo and its underlying worldview that are useful in negotiating institutions and positioned identity, in order for individuals to both accommodate a necessary acculturated existence along with cultural lives defined by non-mainstream traditions and practices.

A word about space: There are no hard boundaries in the practice of curanderismo. Just like the border area it occupies, the boundaries of the practice are fluid. There are concrete, traditional elements upon which the practice is built; aside from this, healers freely borrow ideas, materials, and religions.

Therefore, the individuals represented here are reflective of this. Largely, every healer I have known or spoken with in my time in San Antonio had his or her own style. At the core were key elements. However, like musicians, each has their own technique and method. I often think of San Antonio as a magical crossroads. Because people settling here permanently or semi-permanently are from many different areas of Mexico and the United States, I have seen the integration of material not normally associated with the South Texas/Northern Mexico border culture. An example of this is the use of *pirul* (*Schinus molle L.*), a tree tapped for its sticky sap. It is widely used in the interior of Mexico but largely replaced by mesquite in this area due to its lack of availability. Mr. Madrigal always includes it in an alcohol rub he produces; he spent at least two years trying to locate a transplant for his own use and finally acquired one.

Also, an occasional reference is made to Native American practices in order to demonstrate exchange, diffusion, and influence between the groups historically and in the present. My intention is to build a case for shared cultural knowledge that extends beyond the valley of Mexico, the place most identified as the birthplace of curanderismo.[11] The two sisters profiled in chapter five use sweet grass in smudging ceremonies, *humasos*, at gatherings, and for individual healing ceremonies. Sweet grass is associated with different Native American groups but is not noted in any of the curanderismo literature. The sisters were recently adopted into an Apache group, the Four Winds Apache Band in San Antonio, and one sister, Lizzie, is now the appointed spokeswoman. Monthly gatherings are held at her home for naming ceremonies and affirming social connections. The existence of an Apache band organized for this area is a recent phenomena, but I believe it speaks to the growing awareness and embrace by many Mexican Americans of an indigenous past.

The Inclusion of Ethnobotany

It became evident early on that the connection between the healers is the cultural material used in their practice. Plants, whether fresh, dried, powdered, or tinctured, are a large part of that cultural material. Ethnobotany is not an area of great academic familiarity, in the sense that works in ethnobotany are largely separate studies. When plants are part of general anthropological works, they are usually regulated to an appendix as a list of substances used. I find that ethnobotany adds an important aspect to my work. Different disciplines — ecology, biology, chemistry, and anthropology — examine the relationship people have with their natural environment in order to understand food, medical, and health traditions, as well as elements of culture construction. While these aspects are evident in my work, I keep Richard Ford's description of ethnobotany uppermost in my mind, "Ethnobotany is the study of direct interrelations between humans and plants."[12]

There is a wide body of literature in ethnobotany, much of it concerning the chemical analysis and practical application of botanical materials by non-western peoples. But the selection, use, and discussion of plants can also give us a way to understand how people think about plants that, in turn, demonstrates how the world at large is viewed. The fact that medicinal plants are purchased from a *botanica* — a shop where herbs, amulets, candles, and other ritual paraphernalia are sold, sometimes run by a healer — or a supermarket instead of harvested directly by the people who use them does not alter the significant place these materials hold in curanderismo. From my work and from research conducted in Mexico on traditional healing, I know that plants are an important part of the curanderismo tradition, yet there was little material I could reference underscoring their importance in the practice of curanderismo here in the U.S., aside from descriptive accounts of their use.

My project was also concerned with the following four areas for the data they could yield in terms of cultural relevance: notions of pathology, botanical medicines, techniques of treatment, and the healer's view of his/her position in the community. I approached these areas through a combination of documentary research, interviewing, and participant observation. Interviews covered such topics as instruction on healing rituals, properties of medicinal plants, and the nature of illness. I also participated in the collection of medicinal plants and as a patient in curing and went to various botanicas

Whether the objects used by a healer are organic or inorganic, they are an intricate part of healing. The next chapter begins with Golondrina using a crystal to heal me in the aftermath of a car wreck. It is typical of the rituals enacted during times of personal upheavals.

CHAPTER 3

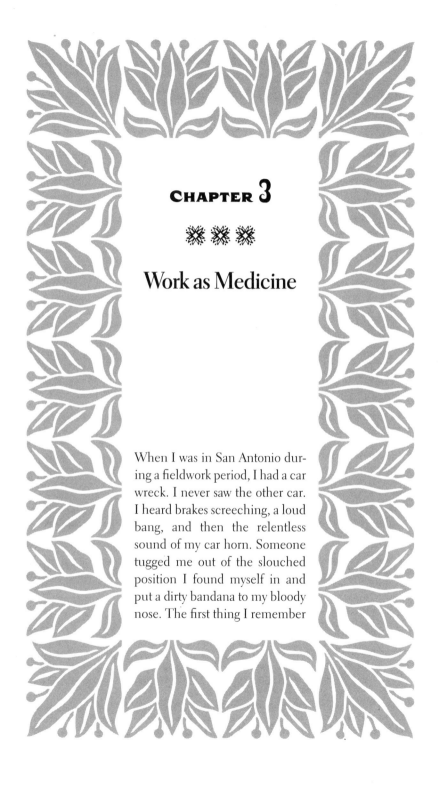

Work as Medicine

When I was in San Antonio during a fieldwork period, I had a car wreck. I never saw the other car. I heard brakes screeching, a loud bang, and then the relentless sound of my car horn. Someone tugged me out of the slouched position I found myself in and put a dirty bandana to my bloody nose. The first thing I remember seeing was Golondrina flying down the sidewalk, or so it seemed to me, looking more frightened than I felt. She pushed people out of the way and quickly began to check me. She had taken charge of the situation. Someone called the police and an ambulance.

I was lucky in two ways. One, it was not a serious accident; two, it happened in front of a shop owned by Golondrina, a curandera with whom I now work. The people who pulled me out of the car were the folks from the neighborhood. The people who spoke to the police on my behalf were those I had seen drift in and out of her resale shop. The woman who called Golondrina from a neighbor's house down the street owns the shop next to hers.

Someone called my niece to take me home. Before letting me go, Golondrina felt I needed to be treated for *susto*—magical fright. I was shaky, and my hands would not stop trembling. She said I was turning *amarilla*, meaning my face was drained of blood and that I looked pale and a little yellow. Amarilla is also a sign of a more serious form of susto setting in that can precipitate soul loss. Into the shop we went, the neighbors trailing behind us, the guys from the neighborhood admonishing me to be more careful. I hollered at my niece to bring my tape recorder from the car; I was not so shaky that I did not recognize an ethnographic moment being handed to me.

We went into the yard behind her shop, and she lit charcoal in a cast-iron skillet. We stood, talking about the accident. I leaned against my niece and listened to the coals pop as the fire began to die. Once they were ready, we all went into the shop. She placed the skillet on the floor, sprinkling powdery incense on the hot coals. I was directed to step over the smoky incense three times in the pattern of a cross. It smelled of coffee and oranges. I bathed myself with the incense. Leaning over the whitish smoke, I moved my cupped hands over my head and arms. Closing my eyes, I did this several times. I could feel my racing heart slow down a little as the warmth of the coals reached my face and hands. I opened my eyes and saw my niece holding the tape recorder in her upturned hand, her elbow resting on a cocked hip. A little frown settled on her forehead. I was glad that she was there.

Holding an alum crystal, Golondrina passed her hand over my body three times, repeating prayers and entreating her guardian saints to take care of me and to help me get over my shock. She perfumed my hair. Speaking loudly in my right ear, she called my spirit back to me, just in case, using my full name: "*el espiritu de Elizabeth de la Portilla ven para atras.*" The smell of the perfume and smoke made me a little nauseous;

the throbbing of my face and right arm added to my discomfort. Later I developed bruises around my eyes, hands, belly, and arms.

After Golondrina finished my healing ritual, she gave me the alum and directed me to throw it out in the middle of the intersection where my accident occurred. I thought this odd at the time, since alum is usually burned. In Spanish it is called *piedra de alumbre*, fire rock. It is believed that the alum absorbs negative energy, and burning it releases the client from her/his affliction. But as I watched cars run over it, the crystal shattered into smaller and smaller pieces until finally I could not tell the difference between it and the remaining bits of glass from my windshield. Then I understood why she had taken this tack. I felt a weight come off my shoulders, and my hands stopped shaking. I turned and walked back to her. She gave me a hug and said, "You're going to be okay." I knew she was right.

I went home and rested, feeling a little better knowing someone was looking after my soul. This was repeated the next two days. Each evening she and another individual I work with, Mr. Madrigal, called to check on me, recommending teas and *consejos*, advice to make me feel better.

I reflected that on that particular day, like many others, I had gone to talk with her about healing, to talk of her life and motivations, hoping I might get a chance to see her in action. Little did I know that I would be the one needing help, that I would become my own subject, the one observed. My own story has become part of the research and part of the analysis.

I have used this incident on occasion while on academic panels. After my presentation people often ask general questions. One young woman offered the comment that she felt I was not objective, that I "liked" the people too much. She was right; I do like them very much. I have a hard time with objectivity, or with what is traditionally called objectivity in anthropology.

That sense of distance and the unbiased watcher, whom I learned about in fieldwork classes, is not something I can duplicate in the field. In the paper, I present ideas of identity and culturally constructed illnesses. I end with my own healing, my own experience.

What I was trying to get across was how a client of Golondrina's might feel after this type of activity, because until this accident happened I really did not know how someone might feel. The last time anyone healed me, in a similar fashion, I was a sick child with a bellyache.

I also wanted to show how quickly one's position can change from observer to participant. Would this woman have made that remark if I were

a fair-haired, fair-skinned academic from the Midwest studying ritual practices in Latin America? Would it be seen as lacking objectivity or praised as
"really getting close to your subject" and "understanding the native's point
of view"? I have embraced a discipline that traditionally has little respect
for voices from the margin, much less for messy emotions. I did not know
this as an undergraduate; then it seemed to me that anthropology held all
the answers.

Going Back to Where We Came From

My dilemma goes beyond the participant-observer paradox because I work
at home in a city which has been home to my family for over two hundred
years. My subjects are people who treat me like family. I feel a daughter's
obligation to them: to make them proud, to bring home a little of the larger
world, and to be an example to the younger ones who are their children
and grandchildren.

Conchita, Golondrina's daughter, related to me recently that because
of conversations with her uncle she has come to believe that memories
are not housed in our brains; they are not internal, but float around us as
part of our auras. When we want to remember something, we pull those
memories towards us and incorporate them once again into our being.
Immediately I thought of documenting this and began to turn it over in
my head to see what theoretical framework it would fit. I began to ask her
questions and realized that I was interviewing her. Instead of relating to
her in a personal fashion (we were at lunch), the anthropologist stepped
in. I do not know if I will ever feel the attachment to her that she deserves.
Her mother and I have known each other for nearly ten years. She is my
main consultant but we are also *comadres*. I have promised to care for her
daughter if she should die before Conchita is of age. They have no kin in
the United States. My graduate training did not prepare me for this type of
involvement.

When I started as an undergraduate in this work, my study of curanderismo was very much in keeping with the norms of anthropology. I collected
material culture, the herbs used in healing, plant specimens, and ritual
material; I recorded prayers, healing rituals, oral histories, and took notes
on the play of language and the diffusion of cultural traits from Spanish to
Mexican to Indian. Much of the early ethnographic work conducted in the
United States was done with an understanding that the cultures examined
would die out due to assimilation, but I never did feel the anxiety that told
me I was looking at a culture that was dying out. Scholars such as William
Madsen and Ari Kiev assured me it was. Culture, as all good anthropology

undergraduates learn, is dynamic. It changes. Madsen and Kiev made the mistake of not considering this possibility in their work.

Still, by examining the early work on Mexican American culture, specifically curanderismo, an understanding of how early ethnographers and other social scientists were a product of their time (as I am of mine) emerged. Their affirmation of hegemony and stereotypes did nothing in terms of adding new cultural awareness to the existing body of literature. Their writing, though, helped me construct a cultural and historical academic background in the study of curanderismo. The authoritative etic[1] position privileged those whose work followed popular concepts of Mexican Americans. Interestingly, they were writing at a time of great cultural, political, and social upheaval; however, in reading their texts little of this is evident.

I kept these observations of the standard etic view in my mind when reading works by Mexican American writers and academics. The outsider/insider dilemma emerged early in the writings of Chicana and Chicano thinkers, as in Américo Paredés's stories of the Rio Grande Valley and his essays in Mexican American culture. The claiming of an authoritative emic view challenges long-standing practices and concepts of what constitutes fieldwork and ethnography. For many native anthropologists, we have come back to where we came from in terms of working within our own cultures and also in treating ourselves as subjects. Ruth Behar has said that we do anthropology to find our way home. It is more than a psychological reflection; it is a purposeful questioning with the result of contributing to the field of anthropology observations and material that informs the discipline in a manner not possible by "traditional" ethnographers. If we are to grow as a discipline, this work is necessary.

There have been times during the course of my fieldwork when I realized that the relationships between the people I work with and myself has changed. My accident marked one of those changes. Golondrina and Mr. Madrigal showed concern for my well-being. Up to this point, I must admit, I felt a professional separation from them. Through my fear, shock, healing, and recovery, I came to understand just how much we shared. Kirin Narayan states, "What we must focus our attention on is the quality of relations with the people we seek to represent in our texts: Are they viewed as mere fodder for professionally self-serving statements about a generalized Other, or are they accepted as subjects with voices, views, and dilemmas — people to whom we are bonded through ties of reciprocity?"[2]

The ties that bind me to the people in this paper go beyond reciprocity, for it sometimes feels as if I take more than I give. What the healers and those in this project have given me is a way to talk about my cultural self and how that being is in conflict with my professional self.

Renato Rosaldo (1989), Ruth Behar and Deborah Gordon (1995), Lila Abu-Loghod (1991), and Narayan have worked to challenge the concepts of what is considered anthropological writing by incorporating their lives as subjects and observers. They do so by calling into question the discipline's dismissal and invisibility of native ethnographic work. Their genealogy is in the work of post-colonial scholars like Arjun Appadurai, Edward Said, and Talal Asad. Their exploration of authority, location, voice, and representation in anthropology add new dimensions and possibilities to the way we not only write about ourselves and the product of our intellectual pursuits but also how we can meld anthropology to areas outside of the social sciences, such as feminist, ethnic, and theological studies.

Because of my work in the borderlands and *mestizaje*, the writings of individuals such as Edward Dozier and Alfonso Ortiz are important to me. Their research on the Pueblos is insightful not just for their scholarly work but also because of their own positioning as cultural insiders. Closer to home literally and academically, Richard Flores and José Limón are anthropologists who explore what it means to be Mexican American in South Texas from an anthropological perspective.

Flores, in his book *Remembering the Alamo: Memory, Modernity and the Master Symbol*, combines historiography, mythmaking, and memory to discuss how the Alamo has emerged as a Master Symbol, by which social order — the domination of Mexicans by Anglos — is legitimized and maintained in Texas and by extension the United States. Flores begins his work with an account of a boyhood classroom visit to the Alamo where he was told by his best friend, "You killed them! You and the other 'mes'kins'!."[3] He speculates on what he lost that day: "Innocence? Certitude? Identity? . . . Whatever it was, it was gone. And like many other losses in my life, this one could not be replaced."[4] Flores asks himself the questions that many of us growing up in the borderlands confront at different times of our lives when interacting in the social\cultural environment of the dominant society. Through his reflections he is answering the question anthropologists have asked countless of times in their fieldwork: "What does a native think of his world?" Flores's book uses the memories of his community, of popular culture, and his own recollection to construct his thesis.

Limón is both insider and outsider as he explores cultural identity among working class Chicanos in his book, *Dancing With the Devil*. In ruminating autobiographically on his own development as an ethnographer, he uses his skills as an anthropologist to explore the intersection of folklore, history, cultural accommodation, and identity shifting. His work is largely male centered. His last chapter discusses curanderas as sites of counter-hegemonic discourse leaning towards a description of androgyny, but it is not totally successful. Paradox is a word that appears frequently in his text and it is a good descriptor for his view of the curandera's role in society. Límon, referring to June Macklin's work on healers of New Mexico, says, "(She) epitomizes all of the *good* associated with femininity; she is knowledgeable, self-sacrificing, nurturant, caring, submissive yet protecting, loyal, chaste, and close to divine power; but the same arcane knowledge and ability to traffic with spirits suggests all that is dark, mysterious and *bad* in the power of being female."[5]

Límon's choice of quotes and his use of the curandera motif reify the cultural poetics that place Mexican women in the virgin/whore binary. He tries to mollify this expression by attributing to the curandera motif an evocative quality that he feels is lacking in ethnography. The figure lends itself to nostalgia, a cultural constant, and is the epitome of the virgin/whore binary.[6] It is the type of characterization that sets Chicana feminists on edge.

Aurora Levins Morales and Carmen Tafolla take the trope of the curandera to a different place than Límon. Morales and Tafolla use the figure of a curandera as a symbol of social activism, or as Morales calls it, "cultural activism." Their curandera is a medium to communicate the needs both of the individual and of the group. Curanderas, illness, and healing for these two women are not just about the healing the body or the spirit but about the everyday contestation of a community in the face of discrimination, socially-embedded racism and internalized oppression. It is also about naming injustices and refusing to be invisible. In "medicine song," from *Curandera*, a book of poems, Tafolla writes,

> Sickness leaves health hiding in a grass roofed shack
>   In a Kickapoo Indian Village
> under the international bridge that holds
> Eagle Pass, Texas to Piedras Negras, Mexico
> where native peoples between two foreign nations
> use dual citizenship
> to ward off dual dangers.
> And health huddles, hides, in healing huts of cardboard and grass,
> never knowing which way to go to escape the madness.[7]

Tafolla, in the verses before and after this one, draws our attention to sickness as a metaphor not just for physical illness but for poverty, war, police brutality, and ignorance-bred violence. Her poems in this collection are about drawing attention to the social body and its illnesses and how in culture and compassion we can find ways to cure ourselves. Morales voices the same issues and remedies in her book *Medicine Stories: History, Culture and the Politics of Integrity*. In her introduction, Morales argues for a reclaiming of history and personhood from that which has systematically oppressed us either through personal abuse or institutional oppression. In her essay, "The Historian as Curandera" she details the strategies she has used to end the oppression of our personal and collective past. Morales outlines fifteen strategies for decolonizing history; these include telling the histories left out of the "official" books. These are often the stories of the poor and female, those disenfranchised from power. By asking questions as in "What constitutes evidence?" we get to the heart of traditional historical accounts, which favor written documents over oral history.[8] The former is the norm for Western-based histories and the latter for many of the people they colonized.

What Tafolla and Morales move towards is an understanding of social action as healing. The practice of curanderismo is an exercise in interconsciousness; there can be no separation of a person's psyche and body. To heal one, the other has to be addressed as well. In the same manner there can be no separation of the individual from society. In order to cure one, the other has to be tended to as well.

Arguably the best known curandera figure in the canon of Mexican American literature is Ultima in Rudolfo A. Anaya's *Bless Me, Ultima*. Anaya's curandera serves as a guide for the protagonist Antonio, a young boy who is on a path of moral discernment. Ultima's position as a healer serves to help Antonio in mediating the tensions of tradition and the larger world. This is symbolized in his relationship with his family, his friends, and in the conflict of cultures that ensue. In the end, Ultima teaches Antonio that only he has the power to direct his life; although there are pushes and pulls that will want to take him in one direction or the other, he must find that place of quiet, peacefulness, and strength in his heart, in order to find those same things in the large world around him.

My approach to the study of curanderismo is to integrate different aspects such as those presented here, joining them together in a reflexive anthropological discussion based on an insider's point of view. Golondrina is not just a consultant, she is my teacher. She is teaching me to be a curandera, and the insights that come from practicing the spirituality I have found in the tradition are something I wish to explore as anthropology.[9] I believe it can add to the existing literature on curanderismo, which historically has focused on its application and in its use as a cultural model of difference.

To reconstruct anthropology in a useful and relevant fashion, where often the colonial voice is the one heard, takes the power of a curandera. As an academic curandera, my focus is to assist in healing the wounds of colonialism. There are other women who walk this path. Yolanda Leyva calls historical trauma "soul wound" and writes, "It is a wound we experience in our spirits, our minds, and our bodies." In her article "There is Great Good in Returning," Leyva explains that in the pressure by institutions to subordinate Mexicans and Mexican Americans, actions are taken that render individuals mute by silencing language, taking away culture, and erasing their past.[10] On this last point Aurora Levins Morales is clear: "One of the first things a colonizing power or repressive regime does is attack the sense of history of those they wish to dominate by attempting to take over and control their relationships to their own past."[11] She continues in her essay that "erasing our past isn't enough, they then recreate us in their own, imperialistic version."[12] And Maria Yellow Horse Brave Heart has defined historical trauma as "cumulative emotional and psychological wounding over the lifespan and generations, emanating from massive group trauma experiences."[13] Yolanda Leyva and Patrisia Gonzales, who also writes on historical trauma, are profiled in chapter seven.

Through their writings and their work these women seek to name the causes for the effects of trauma experienced through institutionalized racism and oppression experienced by our ancestors and the ongoing effects of those actions. It isn't a legacy of victimhood they are outlining but rather a call to name the things that have defined power structures, hierarchies, and the continued inequalities that permeate our communities. These women and others like them use their talents, education, and insider knowledge to lay a path for community healing.

In much the same way, anthropology gives me the method, the training and the voice to discuss these issues in cultural and social terms, which makes history real in the present.

Women's Work

A theory in the flesh means one where the physical realities of our lives — our skin color, the land or concrete we grew up on, our sexual longings — all fuse to create a politic born out of necessity. Here, we attempt to bridge the contradictions in our experience.

We are the colored in a white feminist movement.

We are the feminists among the people of our culture.

We are often the lesbians among the straight.

We do this bridging by naming our selves and by telling our stories in our own words.[14]

My entrance into the field was made easier because of cultural knowledge I already possessed. The expressed phenotype that marks me as an outsider in most parts of Michigan serves in San Antonio as a way to blend into a population that is more than sixty percent Latino. However, fitting in created its own dilemmas. The healers sometimes lost patience with me because I could not readily understand a concept or a *dicho* (proverb or saying), bringing to mind Narayan's caveat that "Even if one can blend into a particular social group without the quest of fieldwork, the very nature of researching what to others is taken-for-granted reality creates an uneasy distance."[15] I spent nearly two years in my relationship with Golondrina trying to understand what she meant by faith.

During this time period memories of sexual molestation by an uncle made their way to the surface. I was traumatized. I spent days angry and weeping. I was at the beginning of my academic career and began to feel overwhelmed, fearful, and very much a failure. Finally, I decided to leave San Antonio for a few days and headed for the Gulf Coast. I went to a retreat house on the grounds of a convent run by an order of nuns from Germany. As a young girl I used to spend one or two weeks at a time there; they were the nuns who taught me my catechism. The sisters left me alone, but I joined them for service in the morning and I took my meals in an adjacent dining room. There, I would listen to them pray over their meals and sing thanksgiving afterwards.

I spent my days in prayer, walks, and meditation. One night I woke up from a nightmare yelling for help. The counseling I had sought before my taking this retreat had been short and non-productive. I knew I was going to need prolonged assistance and was not looking forward to therapy. However, after this dream I realized I had turned a corner. Like a fever breaking, my mind became clear and I felt at peace. I can only describe it as a spiritual awakening; I felt the presence of God. The next day I wrote a prayer that begins, "On my morning walk I hear your voice whispering," which conveys how I have come to understand that what we call God is really the presence of something divine that surrounds us and works through us always. Life since has not been the same in two ways.

One, I have dealt with my past and placed it in the past where it can no longer hurt me. Two, I understand not only the concept of faith but also what Golondrina felt when she received her *don*, her gift of healing. I recognize that what I experienced that night was something I could talk to the healers about, and they would be able relate to it in their own lives.

The curanderas, Mr. Madrigal, and other healers I have spoken with have all gone through some traumatic experience in their lives that was resolved through divine intervention. Further, I understand this now in a fashion not possible prior. Tradition, worldview, and being Catholic gives shades of meaning to this event as anthropology. The resolution of a traumatic event through divine intercession and the use of cultural religious symbols to bring order into an individual's life — this is standard anthropological fare.

But as a native anthropologist I understand the difference an event like this can make in an individual's life; how it feels when fear leaves your body, to understand the relationship human beings have with the world around them as a visceral thing. This is outside of the standard fare. I believe there is a balance that can be struck, a pathway currently in the making by critical feminist writers, such as Behar: "I think what we are seeing are efforts to map an intermediate space we can't quite define yet, a borderland between passion and intellect, analysis and subjectivity, ethnography and autobiography, art and life."[16] This type of work is most threatening to those who feel anthropology will go soft in the belly and no longer be thought of as a scientific pursuit, but knowledge, as Narayan noted, is "situated, negotiated, and part of an ongoing process."[17] There are other ways of knowing beyond the western-based tradition that has dominated us for the last century.

I want my work to be what Virginia Domínguez calls a "rescue project." In her article "For a Politics of Love and Rescue," Domínguez advocates ethnography based on love and respect for the people with whom we work.[18] She stresses that this does not mean an uncritical assessment of our research, or of the people who work with us, or of ourselves, but ethnography that does not condescend or presume to speak for those we write about. Along the same lines is the work by Linda T. Smith, who argues for the construction of methodologies by indigenous researchers as a necessity and an obligation when researching their particular communities.[19] The insider/outsider perspective is one which brings its own set of problems for a native researcher, as stated earlier, but Smith believes that by unpacking the historical process embedded in the creation of theory which has existed to this point, we can understand our own unconscious collusion with colonialistic or imperialistic readings of our peoples.

Treating those with whom I work with respect and honoring their knowledge has done amazing things for them and for me. I see it in the way they think about my (our) research. They already have a sense of themselves and their authority. You cannot be a good curandera without an ego, but this research has given the healers a new avenue through which to voice the ideas. A more focused "voice" for Golondrina is one result. She delights in coming to class with me and talking with my students. In fact, they all do. It is part of their practice to be available to the community, and for Golondrina young adults are special. They are the ones, she says, who have the greatest potential of developing into full spiritual beings because their curiosity of the world is still intact.

A bond has been built between the healers and me. With Mr. Madrigal, the bond has been gradual, built over the course of our time together. I never address him by his first name, a habit formed out of respect, and he usually calls me *señora*. However, on the phone and to his wife he calls me Lisa, a name only my family and friends use. After he lectured in my class one day, he remarked that he never thought he would be addressing college students, because he had never attended school. He taught himself to read and write. He smiled, shook his head a bit, and called it a marvelous thing. It pleased me to no end to see him happy because I had learned so much from him. There could never be a way to properly thank him. His sense of authority has grown. Early on, he had told me that he does not consider himself a curandero; that the calling had never come. Recently we spoke of it again, when I asked him why he believed he had not gotten the calling or the don, he related a story to me.

"When I was young, in my twenties, I thought I felt something, like I was supposed to be a curandero. Some guys called me a *brujo* because they thought I could make things happen, and because I knew when something was going to happen. I looked and looked for a particular book that was about curanderismo and I told myself that if I found the book, it was a sign that I was supposed to become a curandero. I never found the book and that's why I don't think I was supposed to heal. But now, I've been thinking that maybe it's possible."

It is my hope that this is the book Mr. Madrigal has been waiting for because in him I have seen a sense of growing authority and confidence. People outside of the tradition value his knowledge. In having his knowledge validated and prized, his view of himself has changed. One half of calling oneself a curandera is to claim that status for yourself but the other half is to be acknowledged as one by the community. For years, people have called Mr. Madrigal a curandero, but now he is taking steps to claim the status on his own. I know that in part the work I do gives him the opportunity to reflect on how others see him and appreciate his expertise.

Conflict and Identity

The *México Profundo*, meanwhile, keeps resisting, appealing to diverse strategies, depending on the scheme of domination to which it is subjected. It is not a passive, static world, but, rather, one that lives

in permanent tension. The peoples of the *México Profundo* continu-
ally create and re-create their culture, adjust it to changing pressures,
and reinforce their own, private sphere of control. They take foreign
cultural elements and put them at their service . . . They remain silent
or rebel, according to strategies refined by centuries of resistance.[20]

In collecting oral histories of people in and out of my community, those
that have been the most detailed, vivid, and of personal importance are
often the stories in which there has been some type of conflict. In the telling of these stories, the person will often become more animated, with
gestures and facial features growing intense. Sometimes I can visualize the
events as they are related to me because of the teller's passion.

Whether the narrative is framed around a historical event, such as a civil
war, or whether it is a war of words with a husband's paramour, the stories
are significant in that they are told in a fashion by which the teller conveys
to his/her audience who they are. That is, they are stories of identity building, stories of healing, and of synthesis.

It is clear to me that "conflict" and "identity" are often linked together
in the minds of the people with whom I work and live. It is not consciously
framed as such, but a theme of conflict and resolution plays through the
language and also by what stories they choose to tell me. As in the case
of my own healing, the story can convey a sense of coming home and
belonging.

Stories of spiritual healing are sometimes told in terms of the healer
doing battle with Satan. A healer will be called a *"guerrero"* (warrior) at
times. Then there is the language of conflict—plants have "power," "force,"
a divine strength, or a *poder* (will) when talked about in terms of healing.
Plants are also believed to have agency in the sense that they can exhibit
jealousy or in that they need to be asked for help. I further explore these
concepts in chapter six.[21]

Why does the arena of conflict lend itself so well to conversations on
identity formation? In the introduction I gave an account of why conflict
arose between nationalities; in recent history generations of Mexican
Americans, now in their forties, fifties and sixties, grew up hearing stories
of conflict. There was the Mexican Revolution and the flight from Mexico
for many of those whose grandparents came of age during the early 1900s.
The struggle with oppression and discrimination for many of my parents'
generation, and the battle for political and economic rights in the 1960s for
those of my generation, are at the tail-end of that group and representative
of those who first benefited from past struggles.

The messages received by those in Mexican American communities, through the activity of talking about things in terms of conflict or competition, relays the idea that life is a struggle. Struggle permeates one's existence; it becomes a matter of negotiating differences. Differences in language, culture, and representation are reminders that identity can be easily lost, changed by the pressures of a dominant culture. In order to succeed, the message is that you have to fit in to get ahead. Ways of subverting those pressures become a part of everyday life.

The narratives presented in this section are typical of the experiences of many Mexicana or Mexican American women who, in terms of economics and/or social position, find themselves recreating their "selves" in order to survive. They are harbingers of what curanderas/os go through in the process of becoming healers. The struggles presented here do not rely on divine intervention in their reconstruction of identity, but I believe they give insight into the process of coming to consciousness, a necessary passage for those who do become healers.

Ramón Saldívar, in his book *Chicano Narratives*, examines Chicano literature in terms of what he calls "the dialectics of difference."[22] His examination of the writings of Cherríe Moraga, Rudolfo Anaya, and others is one of outlining an alternative method of critical examination of Chicano literature in the face of what he feels is an inadequate method of examination by Anglo-American literary criticism. His argument is that the literature of many Chicano writers is one of resistance, with history as a constant subtext to its writing. As such, existing frameworks in the dominant academic structure are not set up to capture its nuances.

Dominant U.S culture, he believes, uses the cultures of minority people as a contrast and comparison to define itself rather than to try to understand its "other" cultures for their own merits. Further, he writes, "The task of Chicano narrative is thus not simply to illustrate, represent, or translate a particular exotic reality, nor even a certain conception of reality . . . Instead, it serves to realize the agency of thematic figures in the process of demystifying the old world and producing a new one."[23]

Fighting for Space: Resistance and Consciousness

Mary Romero, in her studies of domestic wage laborers and their children, analyzes the narratives of grown children whose parents were or are domestic workers in order to understand the cultural negotiation and identity construction that some individuals go through in this type of living situation.[24] In turn, she produces narratives of resistance and resiliency, examples of how women subvert the dominant culture they are forced to earn their livelihood from while maintaining their own cultural integrity. For many Mexican American women and men, a life of domestic service is often the first, and in some cases the only, work option available, especially in cases of those who have little or no education or English-language skills. Generations of women (as in my family) continue in this venue, the daughters serving in the household of the children their mothers once fed and diapered. The greatest challenge faced by the women profiled in Romero's work is how to retain cultural identity and integrity when those elements are in conflict with the employer's cultural values; it becomes a struggle pitting economic welfare against emotional well-being. She gives an account of Teresa, the daughter of a live-in maid in a well-to-do Euro-American household.

Teresa recalls the dominant theme of her childhood as having to learn the rules — rules of behavior and conformity in the homes where her mother worked. No attempts were made by the employers to learn about their servant's culture or to learn Spanish, Teresa and her mother's first language. Her life was one of restrictions: "no touch." Even so, she relates incidences of her defiance, "glaring angrily at the other children when they tried to make me speak English." As she grew older, the lines demarcating status would at times become blurred. She would be included in holiday meals and was given a room upstairs, thus no longer sharing space with her mother. Yet the gestures made to her were ones of convenience. The room was offered after one of the employer's children had left for college. A place at the table for Thanksgiving dinner was offered only if a guest did not show up; otherwise, she ate in the kitchen.[25]

Teresa tells of this as a time of confusion, not really knowing where she belonged and with whom. In her case, conflict exists as emotional and psychological tension, in terms of her own identity and in what she sees as her life with her mother and her mother's employers. Teresa's story is a common one among people whose parent or parents have to depend on domestic service for their livelihood.

But in telling her story, Teresa does something else. Elinor Ochs and Lisa Capps, in their article "Narrating the Self," write, "Personal narrative simultaneously is born out of experience and gives shape to experience. In this sense narrative and self are inseparable. Self is here broadly understood to be an unfolding reflective awareness of being in the world, including a sense of one's past and future. We come to know ourselves as we use narrative to apprehend experiences and navigate relationships with others."[26]

Teresa could have capitulated and embraced the rules and behavior impressed upon her by the employer. Instead, she and her mother countered by subversive behavior common to many marginalized people. They would speak Spanish to each other in private, socialize with maids from other households, and make efforts to visit family and friends in Latino communities. As Romero writes, "Their other life was Mexican, not white; was Spanish speaking, not English speaking; was female dominated, not male dominated; and was poor and working-class, not upper-middle class."[27] For Teresa and her mother, the way to keep cultural identity alive was through interaction with others dealing with the same types of issues and pressures.

In writing my stories and those of the healers I shape the narratives and give them meaning. I cannot separate the Tejana in me who believes in curanderismo from the anthropologist who is studying curanderismo, and the resulting narrative hinges on both. My status as a native anthropologist is a double edge-sword. It is fortunate to have intimate knowledge of my subject, but I know that other scholars may be tempted to dismiss my work as biased. The question becomes how to represent those whose lives are similar to yours? Catherine Riessman provides a good caution on depicting others' experiences and their representations: "We cannot give voice, but we do hear voices that we record and interpret. Representational decisions cannot be avoided; they enter at numerous points in the research process, and qualitative analysts including feminists must confront them."[28] What this means is that we bring to the table our own past experiences and personal inclinations. We can muddle the stories we collect by confusing our past with those of the people to whom we are listening. Nevertheless, as well, muddling is part of the process. No one comes to a work free of opinions, history, or issues.

Clara's story

Off Commerce and San Sebastian streets in San Antonio during the 1960s, there existed a number of processing plants. They existed around the railroad yards; produce and livestock would go through inspection and preparation for shipping. Loaded on rail cars, the goods would make their way west to California and north towards Chicago. In the same vicinity were various farmers' markets, the remnants of which still dot much of the old commerce area on San Antonio's Westside. Not all produce was shipped by rail; much of it went out on short-haul trucks or to different eating establishments around town. In addition, local people would go and buy fresh vegetables and fruits for their families. It was a noisy, smelly place. The odor from the processing plants clung to you by the end of the day. As children, my father would take us to the produce markets. The haggling of the farmers, the noise of crates being loaded onto the trucks, and the smell of fresh produce fascinated and amused me. I did not know about the hard work behind the scenes, all the predawn hours, the backbreaking work of the pickers, or the marginal profits of the small-time farmer.

The people who worked in the plants and markets were largely immigrants from Mexico or first- and second-generation San Antonians. If a person was lucky, he or she would land a job at one of the meat packing plants that required some training but meant long-term employment. It was into this area that Clara came as a young bride from Mexico in 1963. Her husband is someone I met during the course of my fieldwork. When I interviewed him about traditional remedies, Clara commonly would sit by him with little to say or would function as a hostess, bringing us something to drink or eat, contributing little to the conversation or interview.

As time went on, I noticed that often, when he could not think of a particular remedy, he would ask her to fill in the blank. I saw in her a quiet authority; her agreement on what he was saying was marked by the nod of her head. I could tell she was following the conversation by the look on her face or the occasional remark. I began to ask her questions to draw her in to the conversation. She would add things to her husband's observations, and he would assent to what she said.

One day she and I sat for what I thought would be a brief chat. I wanted to verify some information I had obtained. She mentioned Johnny. She asked if he had found a job. "Yes, he is working and was unable to make the trip with me this time," I answered. I said something about how different things were now between us; we were in a reconciliation mode. She said, "Scaring them sometimes is the only thing that works." She said this in part as a reference to my finally divorcing Johnny after years of threatening to do so. Then she started a story of her own attempts at leaving her marriage. It was the first time I had ever heard of any trouble between them.

Clara and her husband have been married for more than thirty years. He was already in his twenties when he married her; she was a girl of sixteen. She grew up in a small town in Mexico, a well-sheltered girl with little education. Her husband had crossed the Rio Grande many times since the age of twelve. When he took a bride, he came to the United States to stay. Clara came over once he had established himself with a place to live and work.

It was in the area described above where they set up their home; he had a job at one of the processing plants, and she stayed at home with their three children. She rarely left the house and had little contact with people outside of her neighborhood. The way she described her life during that time is reminiscent of the way my mother talked about her young adulthood. A young Latina raised in a traditional household is expected to display a certain amount of deference to her parents, male siblings, and her husband. That is not to say that women are powerless. In matters of the household and the children, women traditionally are in control.

Researchers such as William Madsen added to the stereotype of Mexican American women as docile, opinionless, and deferential. The work he conducted in the realm of value conflicts within Mexican American communities focused on women, who stepping outside of cultural norms (e.g., engaging in activity of self-promotion despite their husband's wishes) suffered psychological distress, bring on a physical manifestation of the distress, and could only be cured by reintegration into the community and its mores while leaving behind questionable activity and conforming to their preset roles.[29] The stereotype persisted until writers like Gloria Anzaldúa and Sandra Cisneros changed that view. In reality, women have had a strong but limited presence and sense of power. In the case of Clara, because of her lack of language skills, education, and familiarity with this country, she felt she had little power and little presence. As she said to me, "¿Qué sabia yo?" (What did I know?).

Her brother worked in the same plant as her husband. She told me, "con la misma colcha se cobijan los dos" (they covered themselves with the same blanket), implying that one looked after the other before considering anyone else. She found out quickly that her life was not what she had envisioned when she first married. Her husband was a womanizer and emotionally abusive. He was rarely at home. On Fridays (pay day) he would come home, change clothing, eat, and leave for the night, the latest of his paramours brazenly picking him up in front of their home. No amount of imploring would keep him home. Finally, she grew tired of his behavior and she made up her mind to leave. Packing her bags one rainy day, she took the children, walked to the nearest bus stop, and waited. Unfortunately, her brother happened to see her and quickly went to get her husband. Both men drove up, and despite her protestations, grabbed the children and put them in the vehicle. Shouting that she could go to the devil, they turned the car around and left her standing, crying, in the rain. She felt helpless and lost and so made her way home, as the men knew she would.

Little changed for the time except that this incident served to embolden the woman with whom her husband was involved. The woman's jeering and taunts now included an occasional chorus, female friends who added further indignities to her situation. Finally, things came to a head in a fashion no one could have predicted. One day, Clara sent her children to buy milk from the corner grocer. They returned with a sandwich wrapped in crumpled butcher paper with a note tucked inside. It was from her rival. The sandwich was made of rotten meat. The note, insultingly written, said it was all she was worthy of eating. Clara snapped; she had endured enough. She told me that for an instant she could see nothing, as if a blinding light had gone off in her head. She grabbed a tire iron laying in the yard outside the house and made off for the plant.

The women were just getting back from lunch and saw her coming. Whether it was the tire iron in her hand or the look on her face, something warned them, and in an instant, the woman and her cronies were inside one of their cars, with Clara beating on the windshield. Over and over she beat the glass on all sides and placed numerous dents in the vehicle. The women inside the car screamed for someone to help them, and Clara, on the outside, hollered at them to come on out and face her. Finally she grew tired, the glass resembling a mosaic of cobwebs. She began to throw fistfuls of gravel at the women as they sat weeping in the car, her bravado fueled by anger and their tears. Finally, tired, she went home to wait for her husband. No one interfered with her actions.

She dreaded his coming home, not knowing what venue his anger would take. Her emotions depleted, she felt powerless again. He entered the house full of recriminations, starting in at once, "You made me look ridiculous in front of everyone. I am embarrassed for you, embarrassed for myself." With those words her anger returned, "You looked ridiculous. How do you think you've made me look? Chasing women, drinking away your paycheck?" She told me she gave him no quarter in the ensuing argument. He learned that afternoon exactly what was in her heart: the long nights alone, the abuse suffered, the loneliness of being in a strange place. She ended with, "If you go out of this house tonight, do not come back. I'll take the children and you'll never see us again." But he did not leave. They did not speak for days. However, every night he came home, and every Friday he brought home his paycheck.

Using Janet Hart's approach in tracing back the genealogy of a narrated event in order to understand its dynamics, we can discuss and begin to understand what Clara's story is expressing.[30] Her frustrations grew out of a sense of not belonging and of helplessness. The unspoken agreement that the United States and Mexico have which allows Mexican citizens to cross the border and work in the U.S. and, in fact, encourages the practice despite laws and regulations against them sets up a system of twentieth-century peonage.

People will work for substandard wages and live in poor housing because of the belief is that it is better than what they left behind in Mexico. For many people, it is a better life. The negative side to this is that the threat of having it all taken from you is very real. One false step, one antagonistic motion or word towards an employer is sometimes all that is needed for an undocumented worker to earn a trip back across the border, courtesy of INS.

Sometimes a person will come into conflict with another and will find himself or herself reported to the agency out of revenge. Like the Texas Rangers before them, INS works using fear. The history of the South Texas area, filled with violence and fear, sets in motion the social barriers that made Clara feel disenfranchised. Her attitude, reflected in her saying "*¿Qué sabia yo?*," is heart-numbing in its simple eloquence, "What did I know?" In one phrase is reflected the helplessness of being an outsider and the sense of not having any control in the situation. In this phrase there is no conflict, just resignation. In taking control of the situation by attacking her rival, she went from resignation to active agency; it was a defining moment for her. By doing so, she changed who she was and took her place in the community, and no one interfered in her actions. While it seems that she played the stereotypical Latina in the first part of the narrative, I would argue that it was her sense of not belonging and not knowing the rules of engagement that kept her numb. It was when her rival crossed the line by sending the package home with her children that she felt compelled to act. The woman crossed over into Clara's realm, the only safe space she had managed to carve out, as a mother to her children. Would she have taken such action if the package had never been sent? If her children had not been involved? It is difficult to say.

She tried to leave him before; but when the children were taken from her, she lost her nerve. Why the children? Why is it that they figure so prominently in her behavior? The children are the catalyst to her actions. Her inclination to remain in the background, to put up with her husband's behavior, was shoved to the background when she felt her children were threatened in some way. I believe she acted the way she did, initially, because she was angry that her children were being approached. It called into question her place as a caretaker, and it threatened her children's well being. But by the end of the encounter, it was her life, her identity, for which she was struggling: "You looked ridiculous. How do you think you've made me look?"

The balance of power in their marriage changed at this point. She would never take a subservient role again, nor would her husband ever treat her in that fashion again. He became the man I know him to be, the one who remembers to bring his wife *leche quemada* (caramel candy) from Mexico because it is her favorite.

What Clara experienced, what she felt, has been described to me by the healers when they come into their gift. It is a time of deep mental and emotional conflict, a defining moment in their lives. There is a surge of strength that comes to them, a sense of clarity and calmness that forever changes their lives. The difference between their experiences and Clara's is that the healers, in changing their lives, claim divine intervention. Not only does their sense of self change, but also they become part of the public domain. Healers lose some of their individuality in accepting the don, the gift, of healing. Becoming a healer is not just by self-proclamation but also by community acknowledgement.[31] The gift of healing is sometimes revealed in the form of a dream or some type of divine visitation.

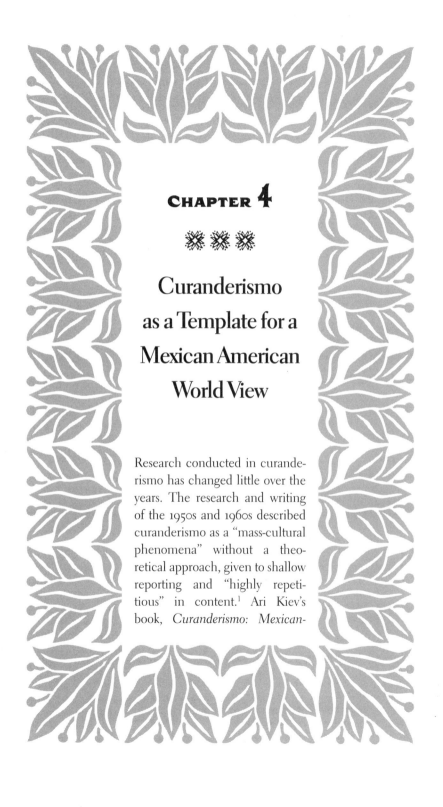

CHAPTER 4

❊ ❊ ❊

Curanderismo as a Template for a Mexican American World View

Research conducted in curanderismo has changed little over the years. The research and writing of the 1950s and 1960s described curanderismo as a "mass-cultural phenomena" without a theoretical approach, given to shallow reporting and "highly repetitious" in content.[1] Ari Kiev's book, *Curanderismo: Mexican-*

American Folk Psychiatry, is problematic because it feeds a stereotypical view of Mexican American culture. Madsen in 1964 wrote *The Mexican-Americans of South Texas* and was credited with being one of the first to use social class as a variable in understanding curanderismo. Trotter and Chavira's 1981 book, *Curanderismo*, is the one most often cited in literature. It is the first well-structured, social science study examining curanderismo in its cultural context, by interviewing numerous healers and their clients. Often, previous studies of curanderismo have been clinical or nutritional in nature and have not described a legitimate belief system with its own history and systematics. If anything, an attempt is made to legitimize folk tradition by accentuating its parallels with European scientific medicine or showing how it can supplement scientific medicine.[2]

The work in this field is most often conducted by those in the medical community, covering topics such as dual-system access and delivery of medical services and mental healthcare.[3] Little work has been done linking curanderismo with the acculturation process of individuals, as an avenue for identity formation, in issues of gender, or other variables that define cultural orientation. In my conversations with them, cuaranderas and curanderos described the circumstances under which they became aware of their don during periods of chaos and personal turmoil. This observation, of a dramatic life experience precipitating an adoption of a new identity in the context of curanderismo, has not been documented. Yet it has a direct correlation to the effectiveness of the healer in his/her community.

In examining the description of *niveles* as conveyed by Trotter and Chavira, the narrative of how Mexican American culture is constructed, how the mythology of a people is played out, and how the collective life-world is approached becomes evident. In their assessment there are three niveles: the material, the mental, and the spiritual. From these the healers draw their power. Trotter and Chavira's 1981 book, *Curanderismo*, describes the material, mental, and spiritual niveles, levels from which healers draw their power.[4]

Through my research and discussions with the healers, I believe it is more accurate to say that there are four niveles: the material, the mental, the spiritual, and the emotional realms. Trotter and Chavira combine the mental and emotional into one area, but the healers identify them separately. Curanderismo also dictates that there are four aspects of what constitutes a person's life: the physical (material), the mind (mental), the spiritual, and the emotional. It is important to note that the body is constituted of these four aspects.

Together they are more than an integrated whole, a sum of the parts. The healers often describe themselves as an empty vessel that is filled with a divine healing energy. I heard this description so often that I finally asked if that is what the body is, an empty vessel. The answer given by the healers in the next two chapters is "yes." The body is a corporeal manifestation of a person's essences. It is like a glass into which water from four different sources is poured. Distinctions of each disappear in the manifestation of the body. When the body is ill, it is indicative of a rupture in that union; one has too much or too little of a particular force. Can the body be broken? Yes. Just as a pot or glass can be cracked and liquid drains out, so can the body. This would explain soul loss, which is an illness that manifests itself physically though shock, fainting, a racing heart rate, and disorientation. These physical signs are indicators that the soul (contained within the spiritual realm) is in danger of taking flight.

The healers do not see one nivele as more important than the other. They are equal, just as the aspects that constitute life are held equally in importance. The healers can access one or more of the realms to enact a healing, though specific training is needed in order to access each one effectively. The material realm focuses on the use of ritual objects and ritual performance to enact a cure. Different materials used in healing are thought to contain energy, an energy that the curandera/o manipulates to counter whatever malevolent forces have invaded the body. In the spiritual realm, the healer enters a trance and a benevolent force (a spirit, for example) works through the healer to enact a cure. The healer is a link between the spiritual and physical world. In the mental realm, the healer uses his/her mind to change the illness, making it benign, usually through the laying on of hands or by massage.[5]

The niveles serve as a template for understanding how the body can be viewed as four separate yet integrated parts. Curanderismo gives us a way to understand certain aspects of cultural life as they are reflected in the structure of the realms. That is: objects and materials contain energy; people can manipulate energy; the spiritual world and the physical are closely aligned and are in contact with one another. Therefore, attitude and state of mind can affect one's state of wellness.

Understanding the niveles as a template allows us to see how life operates and how that is spread out over the construct of culture. It is a way to begin to understand how the culture sees itself and the approaches its uses to make the body well and in balance. Its approach to life is reflected in the structure of the realms, and accessing them is a way to access concepts about the body. It is important to note that the healers acknowledge organic causes for illness wherever appropriate, and research shows that naturalistic and religious healing can and often do exist side by side.[6]

Healers are effective in part because they have a person-centered approach in dealing with clients, and that approach is informed by common experiences and commonly held cultural traditions. This person-centered approach is a hallmark of curanderismo. It calls for active involvement and interaction between the healer and the client.

In this interaction the boundaries between healer and client are blurred. Personal boundaries are moved beyond the healing experience. The client, after being healed, is not the same person he was beforehand and neither is the healer. Each takes from the other and becomes a different individual. Some changes are minimal and some are more significant. The client learns from the healer through the healing experience, and the healer adds to his or her knowledge base by the interaction with the client.

The healer essentially "belongs" to the community; they have a public persona that outweighs their private lives. How they conduct themselves and how they operate are dictated by tradition. They are allowed to alter performance and style in their healing practices, but they are bound by cultural definitions of what is acceptable behavior and attitudes and what is not.

What the healers practice in San Antonio is a practical application of these cultural dictates in a changing world. They help people reconnect with the culture but acknowledge that things change. One healer I know carries a beeper in case a client needs immediate help. Mr. Madrigal keeps well informed of trends in the Mexican American community concerning the treatment of diabetes and heart disease. If he hears of a particular plant or plants being investigated in connection to these ailments, he will study the plants involved and their properties. Golondrina keeps her finger on the pulse of the community and is aware of problems people might be having with their families or of issues concerning the community at large. She also watches the BBC in the evening on PBS and the news on Spanish language television to keep abreast of global events. The sisters "scan" photographs clients bring in of their relatives to diagnose problems; all they require is for the client to repeat the name of the photographed person three times. The name of the person carries his or her vibrations, and they are able to discern problems in this fashion. In this manner curanderos and curanderas engage the world and move with it, not against it. In the coming together of all these different factors — individual life experiences, culturally held beliefs, and the ritual transformation of healer and client —

the members of Golondrina's community survive and slowly find footing in an area that is not of one culture or the other.

Embracing *la India*

While constant reference in the curanderismo literature ties its indigenous roots to the Aztecs, the influences and dissemination of cultural elements is worth exploring. We may never know the origin of particular shared traits. Understanding that throughout the Southwest those of us with a mestizo background have deep and old ties to the land we call home, we do not have to look to Mexico as our sole cultural originator.

Consultants frequently volunteered their own Indian ancestry or their former Indian teachers. In none of these cases was a particular group referenced, but such remarks show an affinity for indigenous philosophy and practice. Don Virgilio noted that both his parents were Mexican Indians. Golondrina speaks of Don Virgilio as having a "warrior spirit," meaning an Indian warrior. During Aida's quest to affirm her powers, she was led by an Indian spirit guide. Mr. Madrigal related stories of an "Indito" in Mexico whose healing practices were sanctioned by the government. This theme recurs often enough to suggest that native heritage is a marker of true power and ability.

This prestige valuing of Indian descent contradicts historical patterns for Mexican Americans in general. But it indicates a move towards reclamation of an indigenous heritage long denied. In *México Profundo*, Bonfil Batalla describes how the colonizers sought to erase the native people's indigenous identity through forced religious conversion, the separation of children from their parents, and the enforcement of European hegemony, equating non-white, non-western peoples to inferior beings. He describes it as a form of domination different from what had been experienced before in the Americas, one born from the reconquest of Spain from the Moors. The Spanish brought with them the ideas of Manifest Destiny that would later be sharply defined by the U.S. The spread of Catholicism and land acquisition went hand in hand for the Spanish.[7]

Anthropologist Martha Menchaca has presented an argument on the suppression of Indian identity among Mexican Americans. According to Menchaca, during the 1800s and into the 1900s, many Mexicans were denied property and political rights for looking or being thought of as "too Indian." The political and social forces at work in the United States dictated that Indian ethnicity was a disadvantage. American citizens of Mexican origin who were classified as Caucasian stood a greater chance of exercising their rights, while those who were classified as Indian were subject to segregation and denial of legal rights.[8] Arguably, for many Mexican Americans being subjected to this type of treatment could lead to the denial or at least repression of an indigenous heritage.

The turning tide is evident in a growing interest by Latina and Latino writers to explore the indigenous aspect of being Mexican and Mexican American. For some it is a battle of feeling twice erased. Inés Hernández Avila, in "Dispelling the Sombras, *Grito mi nombre con rayos de luz*," writes of her efforts to have both her Nez Percé and Mexican background acknowledged by colleagues and family members.[9] Yolanda Leyva, Ana Castillo, Gloria Anzaldúa, Patrisia Gonzalez and others have written about women reclaiming their India identity, moving towards a new concept of self. The work of Rudolfo Anaya, Tomas Rivera, Ruth Behar, Patrisia Gonzalez, and others tie la India to curanderismo in a positive and powerful manner.

Can There Be Harmony if You are Catholic?

The Catholic Church, with its many saints and heavily laden with ritual and structure, looms large in the background of curanderismo and contributes elements that must be reconciled with indigenous traits. Many curanderas/os voice suspicion of organized religion and see the practice of curanderismo as an augmentation to a more authentic and indigenous alternative to the Church dogma on spirituality. But there is no clear-cut division between practicing religion and practicing curanderismo. Mr. Madrigal attends mass regularly. Golondrina will sometimes go with me to a chapel or a shrine, but she is letting her daughter Conchita decide if she wants to practice Catholicism. My parish priest has mentioned to me that parishioners will sometimes bring their children and ask him to cure them of susto, which he does by administering a blessing. The sisters Jo Ann and Lizzie were raised Catholic. The religion permeates their practice, but it also carries the thread of Eastern thought and religious philosophy. They were recently adopted by an Apache group and have participated in their healing ceremonies.

Two important feast days in the Latino Catholic calendar — December 12, the feast day of Our Lady of Guadalupe, and November 1 and 2, the Day(s) of the Dead — are celebrated throughout the city with the different parishes holding Mass and then public celebrations. Mass on December 12 often includes folk dancers bringing flowers to the altar in an Aztec-style dance procession, complete with ankle rattles made of seed pods and feather headdresses. Elsewhere in the city, outdoor *nichos* to the *Virgen* are dressed in flowers and offerings of food. One nicho, in the yard of an older woman near Our Lady of the Lake University, is the scene of a community celebration with people gathering at 11 P.M. on December 11 for prayers and adoration. Mariachis play and sing; people come with offerings and also bring food to share in a meal afterwards. This has taken place for at least the last ten years including the most recent December, even though the woman's husband was in the hospital.

Day of the Dead celebrations, for example, are sites of indigenous practices in Mexican American communitites. One such celebration in San Antonio begins with Mass as well as an outdoor ceremony at the Espada Mission, the oldest of the Catholic missions in San Antonio built by the Indians for the Franciscans in the 17th century. Mexican *danzantes* perform in remembrance of the indigenous people buried at the mission. Traditionally, altars are set up in homes to remember relatives. In my own home I put one up several days before the first for my father, grandmother, and sister-in-law. I adorn their pictures with ribbons of purple and pink, glasses of water, and their favorite foods including tequila and cigarettes for my dad. We believe their spirits will come to partake of the food and drink. Marigolds in flower and their petals line the edges of the altar and the wall behind. Marigolds were the flower of the dead for the Aztecs and the tradition continues. Across the city there are altars built at churches, museums, and places of business.

The holiday has crossed the line to become a secular event. But its significance remains intact. People still go to the cemeteries to clean the graves of family members and friends. Because this day is on the heels of Halloween, graves will sometimes be decorated in black and orange balloons or cardboard black cats and pumpkins, as well as marigolds and sugar skulls. At the Cathedral after the events of September 11, 2001, altars were constructed in the courtyard for remembering the victims of the Twin Towers. Along with personal altars for family members were altars with the American flag and pictures of the Towers. The Cathedral sits in the center of town, an island in the middle of an asphalt sea. On November 1, in memory of my *antepasados*, I went to church. The church held a noon Mass. In the courtyard, people were chatting and having their lunch, pigeons underfoot, and silently remembering people cared for and not forgotten. These altars are vignettes, public testimonials. Like curanderismo, the Day of the Dead has its roots in Catholic and indigenous practices, and it continues to evolve while incorporating the present. It is dynamic and fluid. Ten or twenty years from now it might look even more different, but at the heart of it the day will still contain the original intent of honor and memory.

The cross-fertilization of practice and ideas is not new to this area. Historically the Catholic Church, as part of the colonizing efforts by Spain and Portugal, made it a practice to incorporate into Catholicism religious elements of the indigenous groups with whom they came into contact. The result was the rise of folk Catholicism wherever the Church had a presence. Some of the actions of the church were clearly deliberate: anchoring the cult of the Virgen de Guadalupe to the site of the Aztec goddess, Tonatzin at Tepeyac, in what is now Mexico City; the building of the shrine at Chimayo in New Mexico, a healing site sacred to the Pueblo people of the area in pre-Spanish history. In 2002, Pope John Paul II canonized Juan Diego (who, it seems, is always identified as "the Indian Juan Diego"). It was to Juan Diego that the Virgen de Guadalupe first appeared. Scholar Robert Redfield in 1941 wrote of the blending of Catholicism and Mayan religion in the Yucatan. He commented that if someone came into the area not knowing the rites of the church he or she would never recognize the threads of the religion in some of the local practices.[10]

Less than forty years after the conquest of Mexico, there was evidence that the use of peyote was being incorporated in the Catholic practices of Indian converts. Omer Stewart quotes Norman Taylor's report on the use of *peyotl* by converts: "It (the church) soon found that the beautiful symbolism of the mass was being horribly distorted by the other. . . . They were talking against a graftage of Aztec lore upon Roman liturgy . . . particularly in the case of two plants — *ololuiqui* and *peyotl*."[11] The church's campaign against the use of peyote was not successful, and the incorporation of the plant spread to other indigenous religions. Its use today continues. Reports of its use in San Antonio came from one of my students, who is a Mexican *danzante*.

Aside from incorporating sacred places, the church has also incorporated indigenous traditions. The *quinceañera*, a girl's coming-of-age ceremony celebrated at fifteen, has its roots in Aztec and Maya rituals; further research may show that it also incorporates North American Indian ceremonies such as those found among the Mescalero Apaches. In a quinceañera, a girl is presented to the community through a church service. She is dressed like a bride. The service is followed by a celebration with family and friends. Expenses for a quinceañera can rival wedding costs. There are dresses for the girl and her retinue, food, a band, photographers, the hall rental for the celebration, and gifts that are presented to her. Out of curiosity I completed a search on Google and found over 9,000 related sites for quinceañera information and related goods.[12]

Orlando Espín, in his essay "Popular Catholicism Among Latinos," writes that the rise of popular Catholicism as practiced in the Southwestern U.S. and Mexico has its roots in pre-Tridentine Christianity, heavy in symbolism and ritual. Personal and community devotion were at its heart.[13] What Espín and other theological writers overlook is the coercion of indigenous people to Catholicism. We can view the resulting syncretism as a result of this coercion or the persistence of indigenous elements as a form of resistance to Catholic doctrine.

Conflicts between colonizer and the colonized in the early conquest of Mexico are well documented through the *historias* of the Spaniards. The Indians resisted and could prove violent, as in cases occurring during the sixteenth century in Zacatecas and Jalisco where churches were burned and friars were killed.[14] Or it could be theological, as reported in Spanish documents attributed to Sahagún of a meeting between the Spanish elites of Mexico City and local Indian leaders:

> They began by saying they were extremely surprised and shocked to hear the religious affirm that their gods were not gods. That their ancestors had . . . always worshiped them, and were the very ones who had taught their descendents to honor them with certain sacrifices and ceremonies. It would therefore be a great folly and frivolity to set aside very ancient laws and customs left by the first inhabitants of the country. . . . They ended by saying that it was enough to have lost their liberty, and that they would die rather than cease to worship and serve their gods.[15]

Ricard believes that this was a rare instance of public questioning of Spanish dominance. Native people were not in a position to openly resist Church doctrine because its support lay in Spanish governance and its military. Their manner of dealing with the missionaries was in the form of "sly resistance by inertia and dissimulation."[16] This type of behavior was already in place before Spanish arrival and evident in the power relationships that existed between Indian communities. This manner of coping with more powerful systems was transferred onto the interactions with the Spanish, Ricard continues: "The form it instinctively took at the beginning was very simple: to retreat before the missionaries, create a vacuum, avoid contact with them, and hide."[17] This pattern of resistance was duplicated over and over again, wherever Spanish colonizers encountered Native people. Curanderismo history is a constant reinvention of the tradition. It is influenced by the politics and social milieu of the times. I believe the resistance native people displayed in the encroachment of the Spanish explains why curanderismo has such a Catholic face but an indigenous soul.

The result of the conflict, resistance, and accommodation between the Indians and the Spanish that resulted in a mestizo practice of Catholicism is evident in communities that revere folk saints such as Don Pedrito Jaramillo, a curandero from the turn of the century who lived in Falfurrias, Texas; and El Niño Fidencio, a curandero of great reputation from Mexico, whose followers are called *cajitas* (little boxes) and who channel his spirit in healing rituals. This is a culture of promises and their fulfillment that Catherine Bell calls "a grammar of vows and thanksgiving."[18] Home altars are common throughout Mexico and the borderlands. There are also public displays of thanksgiving in the *nichos* that dot the yards of homes all across the south and western parts of San Antonio. But this is not the Catholicism of Europe. On altars, along with images of the Sacred Heart and the Virgen de Guadalupe, are tall votive candles with phrases like "*ven a mi*" ("come to me") offered by a person seeking the affection of another; amulets of buckeye seeds (Mucana *sp)*; or jars of water and bulbs of garlic placed alongside a rosary or prayer book.

My ex-husband had a habit of walking through the house in the mornings and touching the amulets and crosses I had stationed at the different doorways leading to the outside of the house, yet he was raised a Southern Baptist. There is something seductive and comforting about so visual a practice. The curandera/os have turned a folk religion into a visual, therapeutic art form. The calming and soothing repetition of prayers and fragrant herbs used in healing leaves a person with a sense of being cared for.

While curanderismo is infused with Catholicism, it is not a religion or a religious practice like Santería or Vodou, which outwardly may share some resemblance. Its appeal goes beyond religiosity. In fact, I argue that it is difficult at times to discern which elements are Catholic and which are indigenous, or which are obtained from some other tradition. It is not the dogma of the Catholic Church which drives curanderismo but rather the holistic view of the world that is part of its philosophical foundation. However, Catholic dogma is part of its practice. For Golondrina, a person cannot be healed unless they are *willing* to work on getting better. Free will is important because it is understood as a divine right given to human beings. Free will is stressed in the teachings of the Catholic Church as well as in other Christian religions, in understanding the relationship human beings have with the acceptance or rejection of God and divine order. In western Christian religions, the philosophical construction of free will is the crux of salvation. People have a *choice* whether to follow the teachings of Christ. One of Golondrina's favorite sayings is, *"El camino a dios es por amor o dolor"* (the road to God is [learned] either through love or pain). Lizzie, in her consultations with clients, will often stress the need for the individual to work on "their relationship with God." Lizzie says, "People have free will, free choice. God gave us free will, free choice—if we want to be healed or not. It is up to us to choose." Both women stress the importance of a person taking a proactive approach to developing spirituality.

There is more to this than the promise of an eternal life. Because spirituality is one aspect of a person, what the women are urging people to do is take their lives to a higher level in all areas. By strengthening one's spiritual life, other aspects of a person's being will also improve. The end result is a better life in the tangible world as well as that of the intangible. Economic prosperity is not the ultimate goal. The goal is to be in harmony with the world around you, in all things.

The relationship of curanderismo with the Church is not linear. It is filled with peaks and valleys depending on the needs of the individual and the community. It is also pragmatic. While the sisters, Lizzie and Jo Ann, will urge their clients to pray, and the prayers they teach contain mention and petition of the saints, the Holy Spirit, and Jesus, they are not formulaic in their approach. They do not advocate attendance of religious services nor do they discourage it. They tailor their approach to their clients according to the needs of the individual in tandem with prevailing social conditions. For example, I went in to see the sisters on a regular visit and asked what was in the air. Lizzie responded, "Oh, lots of death lately. *Lechuzas* are hanging around people and their houses." When asked why, she responded that it was the end of the month and people were expecting their checks from the government or employers in a few days. Jo Ann said, "It's always like this at the end of the month." The lechuzas—owl-like creatures associated with witchcraft or death—are manifestations of the stress and anxieties people experience towards the end of the month because of lack of money, bills coming due, and their resources being at an end. This is when the sisters see an increase in *trabajos negros*, works of black magic, especially when the moon is full. They believe that witches tend to work with negative forces most effectively during this period, so people who are targeted will experience a lot of bad luck.

Likewise, after September 11, 2001, there were a high number of cases involving susto. They expected to see the same thing again around each anniversary of the Twin Towers attack. Their response to these circumstances is to guide their clients to a place of confidence and security through ritual healing, which may involve prayer, cleansing with water, visualization techniques, breathing exercises, and guided meditation. Lizzie said, "We're analyzing the cause and effect of the negative events in people's lives and helping them learn to heal themselves and their families. We try to offer them the most common sense approach to life."

The Mechanics of Curanderismo

A spiritual rather than a religious practice grounded in local cultural intervention, curanderismo is communal and individualistic at the same time, in the sense the healer and the individual are in a relationship to better the condition of that person. It is communal in that the healing of the individual is based on community values and cultural beliefs. However, there is no communal gathering for the worship of a divinity. In as much as spiritual practices may be involved, it is not premised on organized religious activity. There is a hierarchy of knowledge and expertise, but it is open to anyone wishing to participate, even those not of the culture, if they recognize their potential to heal and work on its development.

As well because curanderismo is subject to the prevailing social, political, and economic conditions found within the community, the cultural intervention that is practiced in San Antonio is informed by First World values and perspectives. This is the reason that curanderismo is greatly shaped and influenced by the local environment rather than the way it is practiced in Mexico or anywhere else. As Golondrina noted, "Mexico will use what they have there, what they need there. We all have different ways of seeing and learning the lessons we need to get better. We use what *we* need to get better." For Golondrina, getting better means paying attention to the surrounding dominant culture as well as to what the locals understand as healing practices in their context.

In getting "better," the healer is working towards establishing a sense of living in harmony and teaching this to clients. To be in harmony means to stay healthy, to be whole. There is a concept of harmony at the core of the healers' philosophy. Trotter and Chavira call it balance. The concept of balance is one that stems from the Hippocratian doctrine of the four humors: blood, phlegm, black bile, and yellow bile. This aspect of curanderismo is well documented, and George Foster's account in "Relationships between Spanish and Spanish-American Folk Medicine" was among the first to write about its origin.[19] But I believe it goes beyond keeping fluids or essences balanced in the body.[20] My belief is what Kiev, Madsen, and others have termed fatalism comes from applying a Judeo-Christian interpretation to a cultural worldview instead of approaching it from its indigenous history.[21] From Madsen: "Unlike the Anglo world view where man emerges as the dominant force except on Sunday, the Latin view conceives of God as all-powerful and man as but a part of nature that is subject to His will."[22] Social scientists and those in the medical field researching curanderismo overlook the indigenous religious and philosophical contributions that are part of the tradition. Trotter and Chavira believe that it is possible to reconcile disparate views of the world to create a holistic and functional approach, but it is, in their view, a largely European-based philosophy.

> The Hispano-Arabic medical system contributed two important theories to Mexican-American folk medicine. First, it contributed to the idea that health consists of a balanced condition. The lack of harmony with the environment (social and spiritual as well as physical) produces illness, and the readjustment or removal of this imbalance becomes the primary function of the healer. Thus the basic tenets of curanderismo are to produce and protect a holistic relationship. Second, Spanish medical theory contributed the idea that medicinal remedies can be discovered in plants and animals.[23]

To keep a core of tranquility in oneself, when the world around is in constant change one must stay balanced. And that balance is necessary in order to function well, to move forward in one's life. It is a physical manifestation (for example, humoral medicine) and a philosophical state of being. I asked the healers what it means to stay in balance or *en armonía*. Is there a difference between the two? Lizzie and Jo Ann believe there is no difference. They describe this state as "peace within the person; tranquility is a constant calm center," and that "your energy flow is in line." Golondrina used her hands to motion what she thought harmony is, "*es así.*" She held out her hands, palms open and flat downward, at eye level, passing one under the other slowly, without touching but in close proximity. "It's not this — " she rolled her two hands into fists and butted them up against one another. My response was, "Yes, I understand, Golondrina, but how am I supposed to write what I see?"

In searching for a way to adequately explain what harmony is, I have turned to Buddhist texts instead of anthropology. Tantric mysticism, explained by Lama Anagarika Govinda, a teacher of Tibetan Buddhism, explains that, "Tantrism . . . stresses the interwoveness of things and action, the interdependence of all that exists, the continuity in the interaction of cause and effect."[24] The individual, through vigorous meditation and practice, comes to the realization of the connectedness of all things and through all things. In an early interview with Golondrina she told me:

> We have to love everything surrounding us; we have to love every-thing because everything means life. . . . Everything has life and intelligence. . . . when I knew and I learned that the meaning of God is life, *es la vida, el amor, la verdad, la intelegencia, la unidad, el espirit, y el principio. Es la vida,* in my heart, in myself. . . .

This was one of my first lessons with Golondrina, to learn to look at the world as a complete system; to learn that God is life, love, truth, intel-ligence, unity, the spirit, and the ultimate principle. When she says that we are a creation of our own thoughts, she echoes the Dhammapada, "All that we are is the result of our thoughts."

I believe that this tenet, a grounding principle in curanderismo, reflects a mechanism by which accommodation with the dominant culture is pos-sible. Keeping this sense of harmony, of balance within oneself betters the odds in dealing with the often unbalancing world in which we live and have little control over.

At a particularly frustrating time during research, I went to the sisters for verification of details. Entering the workshop, I heard Lizzie giving a reading and watched as she gave her client a *barrida*, a ritual sweeping of the body with bundles of herbs or ritual material. The smell of copal and burning candles was soothing and the coolness of the place helped me relax. Lizzie and Jo Ann greeted me with hugs and smiles. Lizzie insisted on giving me a card reading; she said she had been thinking about me frequently in the previous few days. The cards told her that I had a lechuza hanging over me. She believed that someone placed a *trabajo* (work of magic) on me out of jealousy to keep me from being successful. The result, she told me, was my sense of apprehension, my inability to finish my work, my not meeting deadlines, and general chaos. "How can you get anything done when this is hanging over you?" She had me stand in front of the altar that prominently displayed icons, candles, and scattered crystals and gave me a barrida with a *piedra de alumbre*. Holy water was sprinkled all over me, and she prayed throughout the ritual. I left feeling calmer and surer of myself. The prayers and ritual served to remind me of my place as a traditional person.

Lizzie's actions and the attention given to me by both sisters served to reassure me of my abilities to complete the task. They believe that my research in curanderismo is worthwhile but that it brings with it certain risks. Because I am in contact with many different people I am vulnerable to the energy people carry and put off. They mildly reprimanded me and said I need to take better care of myself by consciously preparing in a spiritual fashion, the way they do, when I go out and conduct research as well as during my everyday work.

What this did for me was help me symbolically by using the figure of the lechuza to focus my uncertainties and Lizzie's card reading to identify my anxieties and apprehensions. In a practical fashion, I know I have a hard time focusing on tasks and the sisters reminded me of that by saying I need to take better care of myself. Taking time to examine myself through prayer and meditation is taking control on one level, but it is also a release, a letting go at the same time, a way to tie back into the larger world. This seems like a paradox, but it is possible. Their actions and words gave me a way to deal with the things I had to do. This reminding, this way of handling the world, is something they try to impart to people on a daily basis.

Some relationships that healers and clients have with one another is built over the course of time. These are heartfelt and intimate. A healer is friendly but not a friend, a guide and teacher, but the most honest ones tell their clients that the real work is taken on by the individual. The next chapter explains how healers understand their place in the community and the people with whom they work.

CHAPTER 5

Healers and Their Clients

Imagine a typical Saturday morning on San Antonio's Southside: Conjunto music rides over on humid air from the flea market's main plaza where food, water fountains, and toilets are located. The bajo sexto's resonating beat has my toe tapping; Germans may have taught us the Polka, but the rhythm is strictly Tex-

Mex. Things are lively for a weekend morning, and the day promises to be a hot one. We sit on hard metal chairs behind a table with rickety legs. Golondrina and I watch people stroll from vendor to vendor, eyes rarely meeting unless a sale is possible. Spread out on top of Golondrina's table is a variety of packaged herbs. Some are for slimming down or smoothing out the skin. Others sport pictures of cultural icons: a bride and groom, a Buddha, or dollar signs symbolizing what the herbs encourage. One yellow box has the profile of an Indian in a long, feathered headdress. The writing on the package advertises the spiritual strength of the herbs contained within: "When you have a tough problem, make a tea out of these herbs and then pour them over yourself when you take a bath." Golondrina often recommends herbal baths. I will hear her dispense this healing technique to clients many times over the course of our time together.

"But does it work?" I ask her. "Sure, if you have faith" she replies. This, too, is something I will hear frequently.

The skeptical look I give her brings about a sharp reprimand. Leaning forward, she tells me in a forceful, low tone, "People want to see something incredible; they want to be healed, just like that. They all want magic." Waving her hand rapidly like a wand in the air, she adds, "And you know what? So do you."

I have to admit to myself that she is right. There is something in me that longs to see magic, wants to believe the incredible. Why not? I grew up with stories of the impossible. In the world of my grandmother, with whom I spent a great part of my childhood, entities that inhabit the supernatural frequently cross over into the realm of the living. The two inhabit the same space. Curtains pushed out by a strong breeze sometimes announce the arrival of a dead relative. A dog barking at an empty corner of a room keeps a *mal ser,* an evil spirit, at bay. The intruding spirit cannot fool an animal; the dog knows when something is not right. This is what I expect from Golondrina: stories of magical battles and miraculous cures—my childhood revisited. The stories of spiritual battles will indeed come and some even unfold during our time together, but above all, what I have learned from the healers is that faith and compassion are the real magic. To learn to heal oneself is to practice the incredible.

Despite talks with healers and a general survey it is hard for me to gauge how many people are practicing curanderismo in San Antonio. Lizzie, one of the curanderas profiled in this chapter, believes there are somewhere in the neighborhood of 200 practicing individuals. Add to that a small but active population of Santería practitioners, charismatic Christians, and others who advertise as psychics. The botánicas or *yerberías* that supply herbs and ritual material cater across the different practices; there are fifty or more such shops in the area where the healers operate. From all this a picture begins to emerge of a practice that is not in danger of dying out but one that is evolving to meet the needs of the community.

All the healers in this chapter are from the San Antonio area, except for Keta who is from the Rio Grande Valley (I met Keta through a student at the university where I teach). Together they represent various practices of curanderismo. Aida is the youngest of the group. She is thirty one and a successful businesswoman. Her grandmothers and a paternal great-aunt have passed their psychic and healing abilities to her, she feels. At this point in her life, she is at a crossroads. She feels incomplete in not practicing curanderismo full time; in her words, she's "afraid to come out of the closet." What is interesting is that she feels strongest when in Mexico or in the Rio Grande Valley. In the last few years she has struggled between giving in to what she feels is her calling and the pressure to be successful in her business ventures. At the same time, she wants to recapture her ethnic identity. Ethnicity was not stressed in her home environment.

Keta is in her early twenties, blind and partially deaf. Until she became a healer, she suffered convulsions. By her own admission, she sought out help from various curanderas in her area, for she found that the medical community could not do anything for her. As sometimes happens, the healers she went to were not practicing ethically, and she was bilked out of a large sum of money. Others told her there was nothing that they could do for her, but one curandera told her that she had the don for healing and that if she were to accept her gift the convulsions would stop. When she went through the process of acknowledging her gift and giving herself over to God, her condition improved. She has been practicing for the last four years, and her convulsions have stopped.

Golondrina, age sixty, was born in Saltillo, Coahuila, Mexico, and has a strong sense of ethnicity. She is a spiritualist who heals by calling on her guides, saints, and beings who live in the spiritual realm. She prefers to act as a guide and instructor, teaching others how to use their own energy to stay well; she enjoys having this role in the community. Her clients, like those of all the healers profiled, come to her by word of mouth. She is one of my main consultants and is profiled in more depth later in the chapter.

Diana is the daughter of a healer and was in training by her mother when the older woman became ill and died. I met Diana briefly and talked with her for just an afternoon. It did not seem to me that her intent was sincere. When asked why she wanted to be a healer, she told me it was because she liked the way people sought her mother's help and advice.

Mr. Madrigal is a *yerbero* (herbalist); he does not call himself a curandero. He raises plants and herbs that are used in healing and often instructs buyers in their use and preparation. He does not conduct healing rituals, except for his family. Mr. Madrigal is in his sixties. He is profiled at length in the next chapter.

Don Virgilio, at age eighty, is the oldest consultant. His name kept coming up in conversations with different people in the community, for he enjoys a very good reputation in San Antonio and the surrounding area. He is a spiritualist and heals by whatever method is dictated to him by spiritual forces. Don Virgilio represents a class of healer very much steeped in tradition. One of the reasons he is regarded well and sought out is that his methods are thought to be reminiscent of those used by old-time or "true" curanderos. His age gives him authority in a culture that equates age with wisdom, and his demeanor is authoritative. His manner is sure and direct. His sense of timing is outstanding; he will draw out answers, lacing them with pauses for effect. His advice is conservative, reaffirming cultural values. Don Virgilio uses common materials for healing, along with the laying on of hands and prayers.

The two sisters, Lizzie and Jo Ann, whom I affectionately call the psychic tag team, have practiced in San Antonio on a regular basis since the early 1990s. I will profile them in more detail later in this chapter. Through them, I met Charlene Beacham. Charlene lives in Bandera, a town west of San Antonio, and comes from a ranching background. She was raised within Mexican American culture, and it comes through in her approach with people at the sisters.' She frequently comes to town and heals at the center the sisters set up in their home. She is the only non-Latina I have met who practices healing in the fashion of curanderismo, but that in itself is testament to the plastic nature of the tradition. She is called a curandera and is accepted as such by the community. She usually comes in once a week but lately less often than that, maybe twice a month. On a typical day she will see thirty people or more. She heals through a laying of hands and freely distributes an infusion she calls Angel Oil. Curanderos use essential oils to protect an individual against spiritual or material harm.[1] Oils are also used for blessing people during healing ceremonies and to call spirits in for help, as well as the usual topical application for sore muscles, sprains, and body aches.

People within the Mexican American community are generally not using curanderismo as a substitute for conventional medical services. Rather, many are augmenting a program of western medical care with visits to a healer. There is a general sentiment that Anglo doctors cannot cure "Mexican" illnesses like susto, *mal de ojo* (evil eye), *caida de mollera* (sunken fontanel), and *empacho* (blockage of the intestines). The healing of these afflictions ties people back to the culture and to the values held by the community.

The concept of fluidity within the body is best exemplified by the following case. Several years ago, Mr. Madrigal suffered an accident that left a shoulder dislocated. He continued to feel pain off and on even after he was told by doctors that his injuries had healed. Soon after this injury, he suffered a series of heart attacks. He believes that because of his accident, there remained old crushed blood (plaque) in his veins, like dirt; the refuse dislodged and blocked the vessels in his heart, bringing on the heart attacks. His *remedio* (remedy) has been to drink a tea made of various herbs that cleanses the blood and strengthens it. Nine months later he felt stronger and has not suffered any more incidents. According to him, the remedio he utilized reestablished the flow in his body.

If a person's equilibrium (the meshing of the different energies) is disturbed, a person becomes ill; if the flow of fluids within one's body is disrupted, swelling of tissue results. Illness is sometimes talked about in terms of metaphor; Mr. Madrigal describes dirt in his blood as having caused his heart attacks, or cancer spreading like bees throughout the body when a person has been operated on; Golondrina uses the phrase *larva mentales*. I was never left with the impression that they meant for me to take these remarks literally. This is contrary to the way many early ethnographers report their findings.[2] The early ethnographers I read on the subject barely hid their disdain and condescension towards the people they interviewed. I found the healers to be very poetic but purposeful in their use of language. They use language to convey the exactness of their meaning.

Golondrina relates that energy in particle form is in constant motion around us. Depending on a person's mental state, these particles can coalesce in the body and cause illness; if the connection between our mind, body, and spirit is not strong, outside forces can cause disharmony. Just as a body might end up as a host to parasitic larva, a person's *paz* (peace) can also be host to larva mentales. In Golondrina's analysis, ideas about mental stability and invasive entities are integrated.

Golondrina further believes that because we take in all types of energy, we use up the energy stored in the earth and do not return anything. This type of consumption is disrespectful towards natural order, and because of it, disasters occur. Mr. Madrigal, who approaches the question of what causes disease very pragmatically, presented a similar theme: he believes that chemicals put into the environment are to blame. From the moment the earth is tilled, chemicals are added and the ground is laced with them. As people ingest food, their bodies absorb the chemicals and reproduce them, magnifying their ill effects. Plants with healing properties are not as effective as they once were because of the chemicals, though his plants are not exposed to chemicals and he believes in their effectiveness. The pollution of the earth is causing old illnesses to reappear, and our bodies are not prepared to resist them.

Jo Ann and Lizzie have expressed similar thoughts. People have forgotten the ties we all share with the earth and no longer understand that in severing the connection we lose a powerful method of healing ourselves. Lizzie rarely keeps her shoes on, as if unwilling to lose the touch of the earth beneath the soles of her feet.

These theoretical statements at first seem idiosyncratic, but they are consistent. They focus on the ability of the body to absorb and reflect influences in the natural environment. Bodily illness goes hand-in-hand with natural disorder. For example, in Mexican American tradition the notion of an unexpected breeze is sometimes associated with the appearance of a supernatural being. *Mal aire* (bad air) coupled with early morning or night dew can sometimes cause paralysis. Maggie, a young healer, related to me, "A cousin of mine, not paying attention to her mother, went out into the night dew without covering herself. The air hit her with much force, and one whole side of her face became paralyzed." When asked what causes Bell's palsy, Golondrina replied, "It is a discord in the body—very strong." She further explained that it could be because of emotions or the atmosphere. Being outside during stormy weather after bathing in hot water could cause Bell's palsy.

Similarly, a relative of Aida's was afflicted with Bell's palsy after moving away from the Rio Grande Valley to north Texas. She believes the move away from his family caused the paralysis. He was frustrated in his attempts to gain a position of responsibility in the Anglo economic realm; the paralysis struck after problems arose with his employer. The paralysis was interpreted as a physical manifestation of his inability to adjust to a different social and professional environment. A curandera would work with him to overcome his frustrations by ritually removing the obstacles in his way and then counseling him on how to deal with his boss. The curanderas I know would probably advise Aida's brother to see the doctor, but that alone would not be enough; his living environment also needs attention.

Holding Power

Trotter and Chavira identify three technical areas in curanderismo: material culture, spiritualism, and psychic healing. In the material culture area, there is no alteration in the healer's state of consciousness. The emphasis is on curing physical symptoms with herbs and common household materials such as eggs and water. Curative power is believed to be inherent in these things, and this can be enhanced with ritual application and prayer.

I often heard the healers refer to themselves as empty vessels or *como una cajita* (like a little box). God fills them with the power to heal. When asked about this, the sisters and Golondrina told me that we are all filled with energy. Mr. Madrigal believes that our bodies are nothing without our spirits; in his words, "We are filled with God." It is because of this that we are tied to everything around us. In their belief system everything around us is energy. We carry it and can manipulate it. We also possess the ability to manipulate the energy in other objects. I asked the healers what God is in their belief system. The answer most often given is, "God is love." While this answer is pat and used like an automated response, when pressed, the healers construct an image of a being without gender, closer to an entity without limitations, a thought as opposed to the Christian God we learn about as children and all that image conjures. For them God is everywhere, in everything, and in every person. Problems arise when individuals cannot recognize this idea. In expressing these ideas, the indigenous life of curanderismo becomes apparent. These are not teachings reinforced by Catholicism but rather by indigenous sensibilities.

One common motif seen in many native cultures is found among the curanderas: the sacred number four. While Trotter and Chavira outline three areas of practice in curanderismo as well as three aspects to a person's body, the healers with whom I have spoken outline four: spiritual, mental, emotional, and physical. There are also four corresponding aspects to a person's being.

The use of material objects — plants, candles, and oils — in healing are part of the physical realm. These are materials that are symbolic in one sense, as in water for purity and cleansing, but because all things are containers of energy they facilitate healing. Healers also exhibit shamanic modes of practice common to many indigenous magico-religious systems. In accessing the spiritual realm, the healer enters into a trance or state of semi-consciousness and allows their being to be used by spiritual forces to conduct healings.[3] This the area in which Don Virgilio and Lizzie work. Spiritual healing carries a great deal of responsibility because the healer is open to influences from the spiritual realm. In interviews conducted for this project, I was told that to work as a spiritual healer, a person must have a very strong character. There is always a danger of influence by entities that are not benevolent (that is, not *espiritus de luz*). If a person proves weak, the healer can inadvertently cause harm.

Another area accessible in curanderismo is psychic healing. The healer uses her or his mental energy to diagnose illness and, in certain instances, to heal the person through a laying on of hands. Trotter and Chavira describe this as the least common method of healing among curanderos.[4] Among the curanderas, Charlene practices this type of healing, incorporating it with massage therapy. Golondrina can sense trouble spots in a person's body by the heat she says the area radiates. Aida cures by the laying of hands, manipulating her energy into a healing power that qualifies her as a psychic healer.

We should note that these distinctions are somewhat overdrawn, in that curanderos often blend approaches, even when professing to specialize. Lizzie uses tarot cards to discern her clients problems and then will counsel them on their behavior and actions. The cards are a guide but her advice is based on the response of her clients and on the initial interview held just before the reading. Golondrina sees herself in the role of a counselor. She will conduct in-depth interviews with her clients on particular issues and then guides them through prayer, meditation exercises, and visualization techniques to help them overcome their problems.

Among the healers, the belief is that everyone is born with the ability to heal themselves or others (usually relatives). Trotter and Chavira state: "All people are felt to have the innate ability to receive spiritual communications, but it is more pronounced in some than in others."[5] What distinguishes a person born with the *don* or "gift" of healing power is their pronounced belief in their abilities, which prefigures a supernatural revelation. The calling to heal that separates the curandera/os from everyone else is not necessarily revealed early in their lives. Power is not transferred from one person to another, but there can be a guide, a teacher to instruct the owner about the use of their power.

Golondrina was not aware of her power until her early teens, when it was revealed to her in a dream. She had gone through a time of personal anguish and was in a depleted physical and emotional state when she had a revelatory dream outlining her power and its purpose. Aida had the same type of experience very early in her childhood. The dreams are marks of transition that do not enable the acquisition of power but merely reveal its existence in a particular person. On the other hand, Don Virgilio needed no such late revelation, saying that he "cried in the womb." He is referring to a folk belief that a child who cries in the womb is reluctant to be born, knowing it will be born with the don of healing and its heavy responsibilities. Though crying in the womb is physiologically impossible, believers assert that a mother can feel her child sob.

Once curanderos recognize their don, they can learn to manipulate extrinsic power. Power exists everywhere but in unequal amounts and those who know how can manipulate it. In many traditions, the possession of power carries an obligation to pursue an activist approach to life. Lack of power and lack of an activist mentality leads to illness. Aida expresses a sentiment akin to this when talking about cancer. "I think it happens a lot to people that were hurt very badly either physically or emotionally and it happened at a time and a place in their life where they couldn't do something about it and they hated themselves for being weak."

For Mexican Americans, power is mainly a birthright. Once the power is recognized as super-ordinary, the person must be trained in order to care for the gift and themselves properly. The curanderas and curanderos are quick to recognize the ultimate source for them is essentially their interpretation of a Christian God. But not a God that is separate from them, an anthropomorphic god, rather, a spirit without boundaries. All of the healers consulted have a strong self-image. All information suggests that to be an effective healer one has to have a strong sense of identity and a confident demeanor. That confidence has to be projected onto the patient in order for a cure to be effective.

Confidence must also be demonstrated in the presence of the supernatural. It is imperative not to show fear. When encountering a ghost, a person should speak directly to it, telling it to leave and that it does not belong. This holds true with the way all my consultants deal with ghosts. Golondrina once encountered ghosts in her home, and she addressed them forcefully but kindly, for she felt these particular spirits were not malevolent but misguided.

> It came to me as a bad dream but when I woke up Tiny was barking and barking at nothing. He growled and snapped as if something were standing in the corner of the living room. Then I felt something pushing me and in my head I heard a man's voice and a woman's. The woman was telling the man, "you can do it, you are stronger than her." That's when I knew that it was something malicious. I thought to myself, no you are not stronger. This is my house — you can't stay here. I started praying hard. I could feel them trying to push me, so I just prayed harder. I called on my teachers to come help me. Then I told the spirits, "you have to leave, your place isn't here. Go away."

She gave them her blessings and called upon her own spiritual guides to help redirect the ghosts. But if the entities had been intent on mischief, she understood that she had to address them in strong language and order them to leave her house. Don Virgilio described an encounter he had with a malevolent spirit that had taken possession of a young woman; he addressed it in coarse, harsh language in order to cast it out. Direct, decisive action adhered to by healers in both groups can also be seen a metaphor or model for how to handle one's fears or troubles. The notion that an illness like Bell's palsy will strike a person who is in a state of disequilibrium exemplifies the problems that can arise from not dealing directly with internal conflict.

Among many Mexican Americans if a person has bouts of insomnia, vomiting, nervousness, or fever, and the origin of the symptoms is thought to be spiritual, then a barrida ("sweeping") may be used. The healer bunches together branches or stems and leaves of certain plants and brushes them over the person while saying prayers. The plants most commonly used are aromatic plants: rue, cedar, and basil. It is believed that the plants help absorb whatever negative energy is causing the illness, allowing the patient to recover.[6] In this fashion, balance between the body and spirit is reestablished.

Sometimes an egg is used in place of plants for the barrida; the egg is thought to absorb the harm and help neutralize the patient's own energy. In addition, in rituals to cure the effects of *mal de ojo*, the patient is rubbed with an egg while prayers are being said. The egg is then cracked open, and the contents dropped into a glass of water. If the person has been afflicted with the evil eye, the egg will appear as if it was cooked. This is evidence that the egg acted to draw out harmful energy directed towards the person. Mal de ojo has its history in Mediterranean folklore.[7]

Another common technique is the removal of obstructions from the body. Don Virgilio enacted a cure on a woman who had been bewitched. He prayed and marked off the area of her stomach where he determined the affliction was centered. Then, placing his mouth there, he sucked out a small object resembling a small piece of gristle that was causing the problem. Lizzie will run her hands over a person about three to four inches away from them, then quickly execute a snapping motion with her fingers as if she is pinching an object off of them. She then "throws" it away from her. Golondrina does much the same thing, with a rubbing motion starting at the top of her client's head. Palms flat, a few inches off the body, she moves her hands around the body's outline, then casts off sideways what she feels has invaded the person.

As in many cultures, water is an essential element in curanderismo. Flowing water especially holds significance as a purifier. Golondrina believes that there are certain ailments, such as *mal puesto*, a hex or spell, that benefit by curing with running water. She makes use of the creeks and rivers around San Antonio for purification by bathing and ritual self-flagellation with river plants she calls *barras*. In a pinch, a shower will serve as a source of running water. Mexican American healers will keep containers of water near themselves and their clients. The belief is that water serves as a channel for supernatural power and as a connection to the spiritual world.

One of the busiest days for Lizzie and Jo Ann is Thursday, bath day. Though their center opens at 4:00 P.M., by 3:00 the patio is full of people. Until recently they received people until midnight or later. Jo Ann prepares a bath water that is used for spiritual cleansing. It is usually bottled in recycled jars or Gatorade bottles. It smells like flowers and has a dark rose color. This treatment is for general well-being as well as for specific purposes that the sisters might feel is necessary. Golondrina will often instruct her clients to throw out the object that has been used in healing sessions into the San Antonio River, which makes its way through downtown. On more than one occasion, I have taken her to an overpass to cast away some captured devil. This is the same river that runs along San Antonio's River Walk, the city's most popular attraction. I doubt it has ever occurred to the tourists to ask why lemons are sometimes seen floating past them.

Beyond the botanical remedies and ritual procedures, faith in the cure and in the practitioner is the most important element; it is essential in order for healing to occur. "Let's see if it will work," according to Mr. Madrigal, is not an attitude conducive to healing. Lizzie will sometimes tell her clients that they need to work on their relationship with God. When the healers describe the plants as having power and spirit, it is the basic tenets of curanderismo they are referencing. Why a particular plant is chosen in a certain instance, as in the case of *epazote* for larvas mentales, requires an understanding of how illness is culturally defined.

Culture and Illness

Arthur Kleinman gives us a definition of illness as a culturally constructed occurrence with culturally defined parameters and solutions, and as such we can say that there are illness idioms pertinent to cultures that individuals can access to express somatized emotional distress.[8] Illness can be a way for an individual to express fear, suffering, and vulnerability in a culturally accepted manner. Traditional healers are, in a sense, translators of somatized distress. They can "read" the meaning of a person's illness in a way that goes beyond the physical. When a curandero or curandera determines that a client's illness stems from a sense of loss of control, the patient is encouraged to become an active agent in the curing process.

The bodily experience of illness cannot be separated from the cultural engagement of the individual with the world. The pressures to acculturate, to deal with economics, labor, and social agencies, can be glossed on to the malevolent forces people feel come at them from outside the body. Embodiment of those forces can manifest as illness. The culture thus defining illness also determines the cure.

This is not to say that all illnesses coming before a healer are free of a biomedical component, but what the healer is frequently concerned with is the underlying spiritual and emotional state of the person as well as the physical state. The healing of the client is dependent on the correct interpretation of what the client is experiencing. Before any healing ritual occurs, the curandera will interview the individual. He or she will ask questions that deal with marital problems; conflicts with neighbors, friends, or family; and money or legal problems. All of this is taken into account in determining the cause of a person's illness. Then the curandera/o recommends an appropriate remedy.

For example, if Golondrina interprets the anxieties and distress a client is experiencing as larva mentales, the use of epazote would seem a logical choice to her as well as to her client. There is cultural knowledge shared by her and her client, and this includes the understanding that the body reflects one's state of mind. The same properties that make epazote effective in expelling intestinal worms are evoked in a spiritual manner to rid her mind of the illness caused by her troubles. Because of the power and energy the epazote is thought to possess, it is a positive step in her recovery. Knowing which plant to use increases the efficacy of the healing ritual, and it gives the ailing person a measure of control and active involvement because often the preparation of the plants as a treatment is done by the individual or a family member.

Using Arthur Kleinman's definition of illness as a culturally constructed occurrence with culturally defined parameters and solutions, we can say that particular types of illnesses need a curandero's attention because we believe is that they cannot be healed with conventional medicine.

There are two ongoing activities when a curandero and a client enter a relationship: one, the somatization of emotional distress, and two, the healer as a translator of that process. Bodily experience (of illness) cannot be separated from the cultural engagement of the individual with his world.

In this instance we can look at the bodily experience as the starting point for cultural analysis. Anthropologist Thomas J. Csordas, referencing Marcel Mauss, states, "Critical to our purpose is the understanding that in normal perception one's body is in no sense an object but always the subject of perception. One does not perceive one's body; one is one's body and perceives *with* it both in the sense that is a perfectly familiar tool (Mauss, 1950) and in the sense that self and body are perfectly coexistent."[9]

Embodiment of those forces manifests as illness. Anthropologist Michael Jackson is useful in this regard; he echoes the sentiment expressed by Csordas when he states that "Meaning should not be reduced to that which can be thought or said, since meaning may exist simply in the doing and in what is manifestly accomplished by action." Applicable to this as well is the argument Robert Des Jarlais makes in his article, "Struggling Along:" "I argue that the category of experience which many take to be universal, natural, and supremely authentic is not an existential given but rather a historically and culturally constituted process predicated on a range of cultural, social, and political forces."[10]

In thinking about the transformative nature of the visions the healers experienced, we can begin to understand what Des Jarlais means in this passage. There are elements in each of their experiences that affect social construction of the individual in a particular way. By claiming divine intervention, they "give up" agency to a superior force and in doing so reconstruct their identity. The pressures from the outside (outside the culture, outside the body) do not make them ill, because the process is cut short by a supernatural occurrence. The memory of this intercession is made real every time they heal someone. They become agents of change.

As well, curanderismo offers an inexpensive, reliable source of health care for both physical and mental ailments. This is not to say that it replaces conventional medicine, but it augments it in different ways. It is highly accessible and provides treatment for types of cultural illnesses that many people believe mainstream doctors cannot cure. For illnesses that are not culturally defined or resist curing by a healer, a person will visit the doctor.[11] Studies have shown that individuals will often incorporate a dual system of medicine, combining curanderismo with mainstream medical treatment.[12]

Ideas on the Body

Golondrina believes that we can heal ourselves in the same manner she applies in her practice. By doing so she is trying to get people to deal with conflicts cloaked as illness. These conflicts arise in the day-to-day activities of people; occasionally, they are not readily resolvable, or the answer is not apparent, and they come to her for help. While these experiences are on the surface not alike, they are composed of and affected by shared values

and attitudes. Her cures deal with cultural tools, religious and spiritual traditions, ties to culture, and community and family, cures which are shared
cultural traits. She uses her life experiences empathetically; she is the map
that people follow to find themselves. We can use the niveles as a template
of how life operates, and use this as a point of departure in understanding
how the culture sees itself and the approaches it uses to keep the body well
and in balance.

Culturally, the body reads as being multi-faceted and the concept of
"who" we are is not a fixed boundary denoting possession. Who and what
we are is affected by myriad outside forces. Much like the passage from the
Coatlicue state that Anzaldúa characterizes as "into Nepantla and then to a
new way of being," the ritual healing of the body leads to a new way of experiencing the world. Healers are the ones who occupy the space Anzaldúa
labels the Nahuatl world. They have the ability to put us in touch with that
realm through their care for us. During healing we occupy that space with
them, and in the process of transformation we take a little bit from each
other and make it our own.[13]

From my observations it appears that more women than men make
use of curanderos, especially when illness is thought to be non-physical in
origin: susto (magical fright), *nervios* (nerves), a run of bad luck, or when
there is trouble at home or with their children. At first glance it does not
appear that the body is gendered in terms of ritual performance. It is in
reference to the person during the act where gender appears. The woman
is often referred to as *hija* (daughter), men as *hijo* (son); spirits that cause
illness and spirits who help cure illness are sometimes gendered. A person
who works in the spiritual realm as a medium loses his or her gender when
the spirit called upon to help takes over the body. Healers have referred to
themselves as vessels or containers, taking on the gender of the spirit that
takes over their bodies. But when supernatural forces are invoked, as in the
manner Golondrina uses, there is no overt reference to gender, unless she
is seeking aid from a particular entity, as in St. Germain or Jesus Christ. For
the most part, spirits are often thought about in terms of good or bad.

The non-gendering of spiritual forces is in keeping with the idea that
the body, in essence, is viewed in terms of energy, and material objects
used in healing are also holders of energy. In this sense there is no gender.
Further, the idea of energy as good or bad has never been described to
me in terms of male or female. Gender is apparent in the stylistic techniques of healing. In the healing rituals I have observed and later discussed
with different healers, males tend to be more aggressive in their style of
healing. They often talk of "doing battle" with a devil. Golondrina once

commented about another healer that he "heals like an Indian warrior," *como un guerrero indio.* Curanderas, for the most part, are different in their approach; they tend to entreat the spirits for their help. Golondrina will sometimes negotiate with the spirits, as if holding a conversation: "Why are you making this person ill?" "We ask you to take care of our daughter." "We offer you prayers and thanks for keeping her safe."[14] She will visualize colored light around a person, believing that lights of particular colors depict particular types of energy (see appendix 1).

Because the body is viewed as a container of energy, and that energy is thought of in terms of good or bad, it would seem that theorists like Donna Haraway and Emily Martin would not be applicable. In their work they speak of how society mirrors science or science mirrors society. They use the language of science to highlight issues of the growing complexity in technology and how that reflects our view of the body. That would seem distant from the concerns at hand.

How does this apply in the context of traditional medicinal practice? One way is to make use of their ideas that "bodies are not born; they are made."[15] What I find useful is to be able to understand the body as a construction because essentially that is what curanderismo does. The healing methods in curanderismo help to reconstruct a person's identity (the mental body).

When Golondrina performs an act of healing, afterwards the client is not the same person he was before becoming ill. He is slightly transformed, psychologically and spiritually, because in order to get well you have to learn the lessons (of healing) the curandero is trying to convey. When Golondrina says we all create our own reality, she means each one of us creates ourselves, our own identity. What she provides is a foundation. She believes that our bodies reflect that reality. The tradition bears this out. Illness of the spirit is often talked about in terms of the body.

The ritual touching and movement of hands and materials over the body is also repetitive and has less to do with affecting the physical body than affecting what the body contains—that is the primary focus. The physical body will reflect the process enacted because it is tightly bound to the spiritual and mental processes of a person. Here, once again, is the idea of the material object's contained energy acting upon the physically contained energy. It is the play of culture on the body, a symbolic reminder to the client of how he/she is socially constructed.

Emily Martin speaks to this play of culture on the body by focusing on the idea of process and transformation.[16] Taking a cue from her, examining changes in curanderismo and its practice over the years can yield information of changes in Mexican American culture and how that affects power relationships with mainstream American culture. In her book she writes, "My focus will be on *change* rather than on *habit*, on processes from which people learn that may *not* have been in place since childhood and process that may contain a degree of intention on the part of those wishing to perpetuate them."[17] The people with whom I work are in constant dialog with structures or situations that call for them to move away from what is traditionally comfortable. They are called upon to have a measure of flexibility in order to survive, as Martin points out. Being flexible allows the culture to co-exist with and flourish in the face of a politically dominant structure that is culturally foreign in multiple ways.

Transaction and Interaction

The role of the curandero is essentially created by social action. It appears from society's need for an institution that is the keeper of cultural ethics, morals, and tradition. In exchange for status or cultural authority the curandera\o "belongs" to the community; he/she has a public persona that outweighs a private life. How they conduct themselves and how they operate is dictated by tradition. Though they are "allowed" to alter performance and style in their healing practices, they are still bound by cultural definitions of what is acceptable behavior and attitudes. They have the authority to regulate individual behavior by the diagnosis of illness that often reflects a spiritual or mental conflict or a deviation from the cultural norms. They regulate behavior in their communities.

Second, the healers recreate their personal identities through a religious experience, which can be viewed as a type of transaction. The following is Golondrina's reaction after her gift for healing was revealed to her. "When I learned the truth and when I knew everything, I felt different. I have to do my own part and I have to work on it and it's gonna be. When you learn the truth, you are free; you feel different. You know you can do anything. Anything. You want to do it; you want it; you do it."

The words to focus on here are, "I have to do my own part . . . and it's gonna be." Also, "You want to do it; you want it; you do it." Doing her part means accepting the role of being a healer. In doing so, she is given the freedom to do what she desires. At the time this occurred, her desire was to have a new life, a new identity. Becoming a healer allowed her to do just that. This change is made legitimate by the religious tradition within Mexican American culture that acknowledges the intervention by divine beings in a person's life at a time of crisis. For Golondrina, life began anew.

Curanderos work to bring a person into harmony with himself, his family, and his community. A healer is accorded status by his or her results. People can call themselves healers, but unless there is a record of success, usually passed on by word of mouth, there is no recognition. Robert Trotter and Juan Chavira, in their book *Curanderismo* have noted, "Curanderos are active agents, in that they take purposeful steps in helping the individual reconnect with his or her community," in turn bettering the individual's chances of economic and social survival and bettering the odds of advancement in these two arenas.[18] How a curandero becomes a healer is part of the process leading to a successful reconnection of the client with his community.

La Golondrina

> . . . When you know the truth, you are free . . . when I knew and I learned that the meaning of God, the meaning of God is life, *es la vida, el amor, la verdad, la intelegencia, la unidad, el espirito, y el principio,* and I learned the meaning of God . . . *el principio. Es la vida,* in my heart, in myself, and God can do everything. And then I ask myself, "What is the problem?"   —GOLONDRINA.

When I was an undergraduate and became interested in working with curanderas, an instructor gave me the name and telephone number of a healer who had previously worked with one of his students; it was Golondrina. I called her the next morning, introduced myself, and asked if I could meet with her. "Yes, but tomorrow. Today I have to take my niece to the doctor." That was nearly ten years ago, and in that time she has been a teacher and a friend. She is savvy enough about ethnography to tell me to turn on my tape recorder when she is going to say something she feels is important. She used her position as an authority figure to chastise me in front of my friends when she felt I needed to press on with my writing or research. In turn, I could be a *niña, mujer,* or comadre, depending on how she interprets my behavior and response.

Golondrina's don was revealed early in her adolescence after a period of personal trauma and questioning of her religious faith. In our interviews she spoke of her father being an alcoholic and of her family's poverty and depressed living conditions. From piecing together other bits of her past, I learned that she was born in Saltillo, Coahuila, that she is an only daughter, and that she has two brothers living in the Monterey, Nuevo León area.

When her don was revealed to her, it allowed for mobility and respect not usually given to women born in her socio-economic strata. She emerged with a way of being in the world, not so much with a bounded conception of self but as an entity that engages the world. This engagement became a part of her self-identification. She explained that before the healing gift was revealed to her, she thought in terms of finality and pessimism. She felt unhappy with her life and did not see much hope of escaping its poverty or the boundaries she felt were imposed on her mobility—intellectually and physically. As a healer her status changed in the community. In being encouraged to develop her gift, she felt free to expand intellectually and to see beyond the boundaries of a physical state. Her purpose, as she understood it now, was to act as an intermediary between the spiritual and physical worlds.

This allowed her to rewrite her life in a fashion that is acceptable to society and would permit her to be active in the construction of her own identity. She no longer had to stay in a home that she felt was filled with much unhappiness. She became an acolyte of a spiritual sect that believed it was guided by "*el niño* Jesus." The people at this center acted as family under the guidance of one teacher. Her life here allowed for the development of her powers. She also learned healing techniques and diagnostic methods. She also eventually taught at the temple.

Golondrina began her training in 1979 when a woman, Doña Nati, ran the temple; she was a channel, and through her the spiritual teachers Golondrina came to know were *el niño Jesus de azucenas, San Martin de Porres, el maestro Jesus, la Virgen Maria y el espiritu Conchita Esparza*. Tuesday and Thursday were healing days, and on Sunday spiritual lessons took place. On these three days the spirits worked through Doña Nati; they (especially niño Jesus) would especially ask what problems were being brought before them. Daily, Doña Nati would see about twenty to twenty-five people; some visitations were longer than others.

The healing sessions lasted about five hours on Sundays; they began at 3:00 P.M. and continued until 8:00 P.M. Doña Nati spent the entire time period in a trance. She would ready herself through prayer, sitting down in a chair with three glasses of clear water beneath it. She sat next to two human pillars, meaning two spiritual protectors: male students whose job it was to stay mentally aware of any malevolent forces that might hamper her or threaten her altered state. She was a cajita, a little box. El niño Jesus called her "*mi carne*" (my flesh). The temple was called *Trinitario Mariano*. Golondrina studied there for five years until 1984. She then made the journey from Mexico to the United States. It was here where she was involved with Conchita's father, a man she talks little of except to say that he worked in *el negro*, black magic. Conchita has never met her father and does not feel a need to know him. Golondrina felt that the way he lived his life was not something she could tolerate nor would she want to practice. She finally left him.

There are common motifs in curanderismo as practiced by Mexicanos and Mexican Americans: eggs used to cure susto, rue for those bewitched, the calling three times of a person's name in his or her ear when it is believed he/she suffers from soul loss. Healers, however, are known to have stylistic differences.[19] Golondrina is not an exception in this manner. From what I have observed, she heals in a fashion that is traditional (prayers, herbs, etc.), coupled with elements that are philosophically her own. She has incorporated her mode of survival and coping with the larger world into her mode of healing. One of the main differences in her ideology that is different from other healers is that people can learn to heal themselves, even in the worst of situations. The curanderos I know in San Antonio tell me that under certain circumstances, especially supernatural afflictions that are considered grave, a healer is needed to effect a cure. Golondrina does not always agree with this line of thinking.

She believes that in our mind resides the power to heal our own illnesses by making our thoughts real. The world we live in is a reality that each of us has constructed, and we are reflections, mentally and spiritually, of that reality. Golondrina claims that, "Our bodies are like sponges, we absorb what is around us and our minds and bodies become those things. If we are negative, then we attract negative energy, negative thoughts, and we become those things more. Then it's hard to break that circle. We have to think and act positive."

When I had the car accident, Golondrina's concern was that the physical shock would affect my spiritual being. She was not blind to the fact that I needed medical attention. She stood by my side while paramedics checked out my bumps and bruises and made sure they treated my various scrapes. She prompted them with questions and had them leave a cold pack for my swelling arm. But in her estimation they could do nothing for my soul or mental state, and if that was not tended to I could still become physically ill.

Getting well necessitates dealing with non-physical issues as well as with the body. Golondrina has learned this in becoming a healer, and she continues to learn from her experiences. When she heals, she incorporates the memory of the circumstances of her life prior to the dream—that is, a dysfunctional family and poverty—and the experiences of her adult life, such as immigration to the U.S. and being a single mother.

In claiming divine intervention, Golondrina became her own first client.

By giving up agency to a superior force, she initiated the reconstruction of her identity. The pressures she felt coming from the outside (outside the culture, outside the body) did not make her ill because the process was cut short by a supernatural occurrence. The memory of this intercession is made real every time she heals someone. Other healers have recounted similar experiences; they, like Golondrina, become agents of change.

Golondrina has experienced some of the same things her clients relate to her in interviews she conducts before a healing ritual; this knowledge becomes part of the healing ritual. She also believes that there are spiritual entities that she calls *seres de luz*, beings of light. These are individuals who are beyond a need for a physical presence; they are pure energy and can be called on to help. Sometimes she refers to them as master teachers; St. Germain is someone towards whom she feels a particular affinity. She brings this spiritual training with her when she heals and will sometimes call on her maestros to assist in the process, but she never goes into a trance. This is not something she wants to hazard. People who trance are vulnerable to many outside forces and cannot always control the situation. Golondrina feels it is not worth the risk.

The Psychic Tag Team

I asked the sisters what idea or ideas they most want to convey in our work together. For Lizzie, it is that people seek out help. In her viewpoint there is always negative energy around, and individuals need to seek out God to reinforce their well-being. Both sisters believe that negativity (in the form of bad luck, illness, or problems) is passed among family members. When this happens, it is up to the individual to break the cycle. Jo Ann teaches people how to pray and will sometimes write the prayers down to help them. She told me I would be surprised at the number of people who come to them who do not know how to pray. The sisters believe that prayer has to be spoken out loud in order to address God (whatever the person's concept of God is) and to talk openly and without fear of what is foremost on your mind and in your heart. The goal of the sisters is for people to become self-reliant and self-sufficient. People need to acknowledge their own spirituality in order to move forward and to accomplish things in this lifetime. "Because," as Jo Ann remarked, "why go out and pay someone to pray for you when you can do it yourself?" The sisters share the same philosophy as Golondrina: people can learn to heal themselves.

There is no "typical" patient who comes to the sisters. I have been present at the healing of children younger than six and men and women well into their eighties. They are charismatic and friendly women. There is nothing secretive about the way they practice. They call their work "cheap therapy" and see it as necessary in an area whose community members might not be able to afford any type of mental health or social services counseling. Jo Ann claims that, "Some people don't know they are depressed," and added they come to them because "they aren't getting help from their doctors." The sisters' ever expanding network of community contacts helps in referring people to possible venues of aid. The sisters understand that the people they see are sometimes in need of the most basic of services. Lizzie says, "We've had people come to us who live in their cars. Folks don't know how to use the system, they come to us for help." Other times, it is something else they seek: "Just listening to them, to open the door. People want and need compassion and don't know how to get it." Jo Ann and Lizzie both agree, "People want love and compassion; they don't have it in their lives."

Their center functions as an exchange station. If someone cannot afford the sisters' time (even though pay is voluntary), they will bring goods to supplement their inventory. As Lizzie explains, "(we) don't worry about the money. It's the people who want to give something." Gifts are common and take the form of eggs, fruit, candles, empty bottles, teas, herbs, and occasionally jewelry or statues of saints or angels. I was sitting with them one day, talking over the details presented in this chapter, when a young woman walked in with a number of empty plastic water containers strung together. She is a weekly visitor of theirs.

A male client built a massage table for their use. Jo Ann's husband is a contractor, and she adapted an electric sander (minus the sandpaper!) of his to use as a hand-held massager. "Better than sex" is what she tells her clients when they ask her how it works. And indeed the vibrating motion of the sander loosens up back muscles quite well. But the sight of Jo Ann holding a full size professional-grade sander in her hands is a little off-putting. Mothers whose children have outgrown their baby clothes bring them to be distributed to those who have none for their own infants. They are often handed out in just a few days. Someone else may bring word about a job, and one of the sisters will call a client in search of work. They keep a list of phone numbers for agencies that may be able to help out the people who come to them. Their center functions as a clearinghouse, a place for networking as well as for healing.

At the center each person is treated with respect and familiarity, and the amount of time spent with a client varies according to need. Sometimes clients will bring in pictures of family members or loved ones for a reading.

Jo Ann will rub the picture with an egg, breaking it into a glass of water for Lizzie to read. Lizzie will then scan the picture, passing her hand over the image, looking at the pattern the egg white is making in the water, and telling the visitor what mental images she is picking up from the photo. Lizzie has told me that the egg is not really necessary but that people believe her more readily if it seems that whatever is wrong is manifesting itself physically. She uses her mind to read a person or the photo, whichever the case may be.

The Sisters at Work and a Story of Hope

An *abuela* came in with her daughter and the daughter's husband. She walked past the waiting area and took an empty seat near the table where we were sitting. She sat quietly, staring into the distance, her lower lip hanging down a little. Her gray hair was mussed. It was shorter than I am used to seeing on old women, and she seemed slightly unaware of all the talk around her. She had the beautiful brown color of an india, but her face was severely lined. She wore knit pants, a nondescript blouse, and a lightweight jacket. It was her vacant look that intrigued me; there was resignation in her eyes. Jo Ann, without being told, stood up from her seat and our conversation, leaving me to observe the room. Lizzie sat with a woman whose face read of better times. She had a hard look about her. I knew that her fingertips would be yellow from too many cigarettes. The tarot cards spread out in front of the two of them, Lizzie was half-interpreting, half-lecturing the woman on her behavior. The woman hung on her words, nodding in guilt and acquiescence.

Jo Ann, I knew, was listening, but she didn't pay attention to her sister. She was rummaging through the herbs, looking for rue or romero. I was unable to see the package. She started a coal in a small hand-held chimenea, blew onto the ember softly, and laid the dry herb inside. Wispy white smoke rose from the top. The smell of the plant was lost to me; there were too many odors vying for my attention. Meanwhile, Lizzie continued with her client: "You need to take care of yourself, for your children . . ." her voice, in Spanish and English, was sing-song, cajoling and reprimanding in turn.

Jo Ann looked over to me and simply said, "Susto." It told me much about the old woman. The abuela was lost, frightened; her spirit had retreated into a corner of her being; that would account for her empty look. "Okay, *amá*, let's see if we can get you to feel better." She took the woman by the arm, helping her to her feet. Off came her jacket. Jo Ann placed a red cloth over the woman's head, and with a bundle of short, dried grass and stems, she began to tap the woman all over her body, her lips moving in prayer the whole time. The woman gave herself over to Jo Ann, her body limp, her hands falling heavily against her after Jo Ann raised each one to lightly tap the palms. After the bundle came the incense. She washed the woman with smoke, over and over in a circular pattern; the cloth never moved except when an occasional sigh escaped the abuela.

Lizzie looked towards the pair and used a mirror that reflected light from the lamp on the table towards them. The light jumped off the mirror in circular patterns, spotlighting the woman. It hit the ceiling, the walls, the crucifix on the altar, and then focused on the two women. For Lizzie the light was energy, and she was sending help to her sister. They worked in unison, these two, even when both were busy with different people.

I felt myself detach slightly from the scene, trying to memorize all the details. The room had been painted recently; a simple whitewash, but it was needed. The smoke from burning candles leaves behind soot marks on the walls. The occasional painting and moving of articles gives the room a fresh feel to it. The sisters did their spring cleaning early this time; the altar was moved from the south wall to the north. Many of the statues, charms, and religious memorabilia were removed and stored. People are very generous and often bring religious articles as personal tokens for the sisters or to be placed on the altar. It is a practice seen in Catholic shrines where tokens are often left as a form of thanksgiving for answered prayers. There is one window with an air-conditioning unit in the bottom half, and a single door leading to the outside. The lamp on the table, the filtered sunlight, and the candles provided light.

I reacted physically to the work Jo Ann was conducting. The hair on my neck and arms stood on end. I realized that what I was witnessing was our history being retold. Jo Ann was conducting the same ritual countless of women and men have enacted over the course of centuries. Amidst the ringing phone, the oldies playing on the radio, and the sound of planes leaving the airbase nearby, there is this quiet, peaceful circle of love. Jo Ann raised her arms over and over, draping smoke on the cloth-covered woman. The old woman stood quietly. She had faith in the actions of the healer.

We are all tied together through time by this piece of red cloth. Red is the color of protection, a strong color that needs delicate handling. It is the color that wards off witches and envy. It is the color of the passion of Jesus; it is the color of the *frijolillo*, the seed of the mountain laurel (*Sophora secundin flora*) which is carried by native people throughout the Southwest and Latin America for spiritual protection. I was struck that Jo Ann would use it. It meant that the woman was quite ill.

When she was done, the old woman was helped with her jacket. She reached into her pocket, pulling out several crumpled dollar bills. Jo Ann busily put things away — the herbs, the chimenea — and I watched as the old woman folded together a few dollar bills and dropped them into the fishbowl kept on the table for donations. She never once looked at Lizzie or me. Jo Ann hugged her and told her she'd see her in two weeks.

On a later visit Jo Ann explained that the woman had a daughter who died unexpectedly, and she felt her spirit in the house. In addition, the daughter's children were sent to live with her, and her resources were spread thin in an attempt to care for them. So not only was she dealing with her daughter's death, but, on a limited income, was now having to raise several children.

The old woman comes in once every two weeks. Jo Ann is working with her, trying to ease all the many transitions with which she's having to deal. The woman did not look any different to me after the ritual than when she first entered. But to look at it from another perspective, once every two weeks, the abuela can leave her house, which she feels her daughter's spirit will not leave, and someone pays attention to her and sees to her welfare. Jo Ann believes that the young woman's ghost is really a manifestation of the older woman's anxieties. By working with her and treating her with familiar healing articles, Jo Ann is communicating an unspoken message that the abuela knows she is not alone during this difficult period of transition.

When I gave Jo Ann this section to read, she told me that she felt it was not complete, that my observations were short-sighted because I had not observed the abuela from the beginning of her visits. Jo Ann explained, "She does feel different, her spirits are uplifted. She knows that her daughter is at peace; therefore, she is at peace. She's making a good transition; she knows that she is now a mother, not a grandmother. She is able to accept the role of mother instead of grandmother and that makes her strong." As of this writing, the grandmother, now mother, no longer needs the help of the sisters. She is on her own.

Gauging by their crowded waiting area and the familiarity with which their clients greet them, the sisters are very successful. Esperanza, a woman in her early forties, is a regular patron, once a week or so for the past seven years. We sat outside under a patio umbrella, talking for about thirty minutes while people made their way into the garage. Esperanza came to the sisters by way of a third party, a friend of her sister's; she has nine siblings. Her mother also came to seek the sisters' advice, as did Esperanza's children. When she first came to the sisters it was because she had financial problems and was not getting along with her in-laws. Lizzie suggested she give her house a *limpia* with vinegar and water (see appendix 1). Esperanza then brought her husband and children to see Lizzie and Jo Ann for limpias and consejos. After that her husband's business improved, and she grew confident in her dealings with his family. Her siblings now come. When her husband injured his leg and it did not heal with the treatment given to him at University Hospital, he came to Charlene for some of her angel oil. He eventually healed; Esperanza believes his healing was more through the efforts of Charlene than of the doctors at the hospital.

Esperanza does not see a conflict in being a practicing Catholic and coming to see the sisters, or seeking conventional medical help and seeking help from the women. For her Lizzie is a guide, and she has faith that the sisters have her best interests at heart. She sometimes brings her children if she has a discipline problem with them. Lizzie helps her by backing her up. I have seen this more than once when visiting the sisters. The parents will bring in their child or children, and Lizzie reads their cards. Jo Ann heals them, and they get a short lecture while the parents stand behind them the whole time. It is reminiscent to me of certain Pueblo ritual activities where the community sanctions an individual, correcting his or her behavior. Lizzie, in her role as a cultural authority figure, is reintegrating the young person into the community and towards acceptable norms. When I was young, it was not unusual for my behavior and that of my siblings and cousins to be corrected by my mother's sisters. They worked in unison to raise us. Lizzie, Jo Ann, and Esperanza are continuing this practice in their own manner. The framework of *compadrazgo* is still very much in place within the culture.[20]

When Esperanza's mother died, her sisters began to lean heavily on her. This had been one of her fears. She felt compassionate and wanted to help, but she was afraid of being overwhelmed by the responsibility.

"So, what did you do? How did Lizzie and Jo Ann help?" I asked her.

"Before coming to them," she answered, "I was like, I would give anything away. I expected nothing in return. I helped my sister buy clothes, went into debt, bailed their kids out of jail. *Estaba muy mensa* (a real idiot). Now, no." She shook her head and smiled, "No more. I'm not the same person I was back then. I won't give handouts. I listen, but I don't try to solve their problems. *No me dejo (I* won't allow myself to be taken advantage of)." It is her smile I remember and the look on her face when she said she was a different person now. She looked confident.

The healers function as teachers, spiritual guides, and health service providers. In this chapter I provided profiles of the healers I often consulted. I provided a more detailed analysis of two sisters who are curanderas — Lizzie and Jo Ann — and, of course, of their clients.

What ties the healers together in the course of their work are plants. Plants are medicine, food, and transmitters of energy. They can be jealous, fussy, difficult to train, and some even seem to know the touch of their caretaker. Plants are the thing all healers, regardless of specialty, make use of. In the following chapter I explore the herbs and plants that the healers and community use.

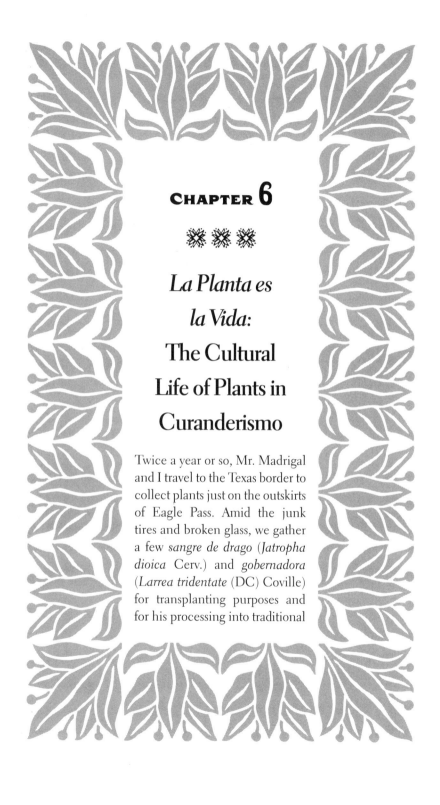

CHAPTER **6**

✳ ✳ ✳

La Planta es la Vida: The Cultural Life of Plants in Curanderismo

Twice a year or so, Mr. Madrigal and I travel to the Texas border to collect plants just on the outskirts of Eagle Pass. Amid the junk tires and broken glass, we gather a few *sangre de drago* (*Jatropha dioica* Cerv.) and *gobernadora* (*Larrea tridentate* (DC) Coville) for transplanting purposes and for his processing into traditional medicines, taking care to leave plenty behind for reproduction. We always go to the same place, and we take the opportunity to cross over into Piedras Negras on the Coahuila side of Mexico. It is a three-hour drive, more or less, from San Antonio, and I always learn something new from him on our trips. He tells me stories from his youth — his many crossings, his days as a union organizer. Time and again we'll take note of what has emerged from the ground and what is no longer there. We know the road so well that at fifty miles per hour he can spot whether a particular plant is growing alongside the road. If it is, we will stop on the way back to harvest it. One day in February we parked our vehicle close to the border on the Texas side and took the time to walk across the bridge into Mexico. It was a lovely day, warm with a prelude of spring hanging in the sunshine. There were many vehicles waiting at the crossing; the current national climate has made coming and going more than the everyday experience it had been. Walking seemed easier, and it was a good way to warm our bones after the chilly morning ride. The bridge joining the two countries is imposing. It hangs high over the Rio Grande/Río Bravo. There are at least six lanes of highway, three on either side for traffic. Vendors walk near the vehicles on the Mexico side, taking advantage of the slow moving traffic to sell candy, bottled water, gum, toys, and other small items. There are no vendors on the American side. It can take up to two hours to cross back into the U.S. on a busy day. Sidewalks line either side of the asphalt; chain link fencing embedded in concrete walls rises high above the crowds; barbed wire spirals on top in a delicate balancing act. This corridor of asphalt, concrete, and wire links two nations together in a very real fashion. You can almost forget that you are suspended high above the ground until you look past the wire at the river below. The asphalt and concrete raise the temperature, and suddenly the day is hot and dusty. The river is its usual brown-green; turtles sun themselves on rocks that rise above shallow places; the water moves around them on its journey to the sea. *Carrizo*, river reeds, are on either side; but what I notice is the lack of grass along the banks. Nothing grows here, testament to the constant back and forth of human activity or to the Border Patrol's deforestation efforts. The Border Patrol moves up and down the riverbank more for effect than anything else. Despair is palpable to anyone aware of our joint history, its tension, and longing rise from the river.

As we crossed, Mr. Madrigal made the remark that the last time he walked across the border was as a young man coming into the U.S. I said to him, "You left as a citizen of one country and are coming back as the citizen of another; you've lived two lives." It was an offhand remark. He said nothing in response, but I could tell he was thinking about it. Piedras Negras is an old haunt of his. He had spent his youth here, brawling, drinking, and working—a union man with little education, not much going for him except a strong instinct to survive. His father was an American citizen; therefore, it should have made claiming citizenship a simple task. Such was not the case. His father abandoned his Mexican family. In a scenario that has played itself out over the borderlands too many times to count, it was left up to Jacinto to make his own way. He came here as an "illegal," a living paradox because of his parentage, belonging and not belonging at the same time. We talked about this as we made our way to the market in Piedras, where he bought herbs for himself and candy for his wife. It was near Valentine's Day, and he could not go home empty-handed.

He told me of knowing where his father lived, somewhere on the other side of Austin, and of asking through family for help from his father. It was not forthcoming. He did not have other family members who helped, so the crossing had to be on his own. He was caught more than once and deported; finally, on one trip at the age of fifteen, he wasn't caught. He managed to stay here, and a new life began.

When it came time to marry, it was a girl from Coahuila he courted and wed. He remained close to Mexico over the years because of family. His mother remained in Villa Fuente Coahuila, where he grew up. It was his mother who taught him the use of plants; she learned it from her father. But after his mother died, his trips to Mexico were infrequent and finally stopped. He said he does not feel a need to go to Mexico; it is not his home. He has lived in the U.S. for over forty years, never learning English but working in the construction business successfully for most of his adult life.

The Changing Landscape of the U.S. and Mexico

Back at the dumpsite on the U.S. side, Mr. Madrigal quickly digs up the plants he needs. I help by bringing five-gallon buckets to him from the back of the truck. We bring water with us to keep the plants from suffering too much on their return journey. I take a plant survey to note the changes from our last trip out and photograph our harvest. I can see the border from the rise where the plants grow; the flags of the United States and Mexico marking the political borders wave in the distance. The days are usually hazy. The *maquiladoras* in Piedras, many owned by U.S. firms, produce a great deal of pollution. The sky never seems clear, and it is hard to distinguish one flag from the other. It is ironic that such a dirty strip of land and water can yield so much medicine. It remains to be seen how much longer the earth can continue to produce the plants we seek when the U.S. and Mexico seem intent on killing the river. An INS patrol agent makes an occasional pass through the area as we go about our business. I always feel a little anxious when I see the green and tan vehicles of *la migra*, but Mr. Madrigal treats them as a matter of course. Our work continues easily, talk seems unnecessary after our years together. Our day ends early in the afternoon.

We watch the landscape change from rural to urban as we make our way back to the city. Every few miles I spot an eagle or a hawk scouting the area from a mesquite tree. Once, one swooped down in front of us, grabbing a dead rabbit from the road. Before I could react, it was off again. Mr. Madrigal commented how scarce the plants we collected had become in the last thirty years. Once, in Mexico and in places along the Texas border, plants could be freely gathered with the underlying confidence that in the following year more of their kind would return. Gathering areas are now fenced in or developed and no longer yield the scarcer varieties of plants we harvested on our trip.

We locate the places we gather by memory because no written account of their whereabouts exists. The landscape is also of cultural significance. One of our gathering places near a creek is used for ritual spiritual cleansing by people in the surrounding area. Near it grows *estafiate,* prized for curing a wide variety of gastrointestinal ailments. It is a popular plant and might be part of the reason the creek enjoys a reputation as a place of healing. Mr. Madrigal believes that because the plant grows wild its healing properties are stronger, because it has no human care, just the sun and the water to watch over it.

When a job accident damaged his back and he could no longer work in construction, Mr. Madrigal turned to *la yerbería.* It is both therapy and a way to earn a little extra income. Now his life is governed by the seasons and the time of day. February through May is the busiest time. February is planting season. Hardy plants, such as rosemary and rue that sell easily, are started during this time. During March and April the more tender plants go out: basil, chile, borage, tomatoes, and the flowering plants (ornamentals). They begin and continue to sell through the relatively cool days of May. The heat of summer slows things down, and then the fall brings things up again for a while. Winter is preparation time and a period of keeping the cold at bay from his most delicate plants.

His days are habitually structured also. Early mornings are for watering and feeding, afternoons for napping, and evenings for maintenance work on the garden and making the *medicinas*. On Wednesdays, Fridays, and the weekends, he sells his plants and household goods at a flea market. He makes enough money to keep his household going and is meticulous at keeping records of transactions, plantings, and rates of production.

Mr. Madrigal is an expert in all things botanical. For him plants are more than a way to treat an illness; they are the essence of life itself. The community acknowledges him as a curandero, though he prefers the title of *yerbero*. In the last year since taking up my post he, Golondrina, and the sisters occasionally came and lectured to my classes. Everyone benefited from this. The students were full of questions, and the healers felt this was part of their calling—to make others, especially young people, aware of their cultural heritage.

The Cultural Life of Plants

In this chapter I focus on how plants fit into the tradition of curanderismo, in particular how plants are thought of. Though plants are utilized on a regular basis by all healers, no matter what their overarching technique may be, people like Mr. Madrigal are specialists. Other curandera/os defer to them as such.

There are several heavily utilized plants. Among them: rue (*Ruta graveolens* L.), epazote, wormseed (*Chenopodium ambrosiodes* L.), basil (*Ocimum basilicum* L.), and rosemary (*Rosmarinus officinalis* L.). Though they are non-natives, their use in Mexican traditional medicine is well documented for a variety of ailments such as earaches, gastro-intestinal illnesses, insomnia, and headaches.[1] By extension of people and culture, similar use of these plants in South Texas and other U. S.-Mexico border areas is also well known.[2]

Historically there is a tradition of ethnobotanical studies in the Southwest, including the work of Carlson and Jones, who studied the ethnobotany of the indigenous people in Oklahoma circa 1939, and Frank Cushing with the Zuni in the 1800s.[3] These works leaned heavily on collecting and describing the material culture of the people studied, precursors to the body of work that embraces a synthesis of cultural and social environment with the geographical landscape of the people discussed. Works of this nature include Gary Nabhan, Maragarita Kay, and Nina Etkin's edited volume, *Eating on the Wild Side*.[4] These works serve as examples of how the interaction of people and their environment are being studied currently. The work I do is along the same lines. Unlike the largely rural setting of many ethnobotanical studies, I believe there is as much complexity to the study of people-environment interaction in urban places as can be seen in the works mentioned here.

Botanical material is readily available in San Antonio, and I would estimate there are at least fifty shops that specialize in their sale. Many of the large supermarkets sell dried plant material as well as a limited amount of ritual material. Golondrina will send me to La Fiesta grocery store to buy candles because they are cheaper there than at the botánicas. Flea markets are often a source for green and dried plants, but some of the more common ones are found in nurseries or are grown from cuttings. In nearly all the homes of clients I have visited, there is *aloe vera* (Aloe *barbadensis* Miller), rosemary, or epazote growing in the yard. The curanderos often have several of each type growing, as well as rue and basil. These they use in their practice and in keeping with their belief that plants like rue, basil, and rosemary keep malevolent spirits from nearing the home.

Transmittal of plant use and knowledge by non-healers is often intergenerational and traditional. Those interviewed refer to learning which plant to use from a parent or grandparent, or the information came from a friend. The healers gain their knowledge from being apprenticed to an individual who is a tradition bearer or, in a few cases, in some type of group setting. Mr. Madrigal, Golondrina, the sisters, and other healers I have consulted each have their own distinct method of healing. Mr. Madrigal uses plants. The others use prayer, counseling, and the ritual material. Their techniques vary. While Golondrina and other curanderas use plant material in their practice, they will often use a single plant or a special combination of plants and incense in a healing ritual.

Mr. Madrigal often uses plants in combinations, depending on the illness and its severity. Of all the people I have met so far, his expertise and knowledge of plants is the most extensive. He grows and processes much of his own material, both for personal use and for its sale. His plant stand at a weekend flea market is patronized by curanderos as well as nonspecialists. He also experiments with different plants, constantly trying for a combination that he describes as "*superbueno*"—plants whose properties complement one another and will be of greater benefit as a result. A tea he sells as a tonic for people who are diabetic is an infusion of thirteen plants, among them pecan bark (*Juglans* spp.), giant hyssop (*Agastache mexcianum*), magnolia (*Magnolia grandiflora*), aloe vera, and horehound (*Marrubium vulgare* L.). He bases his selection of plants on what he has known to be effective, published material, and information shared with clients and other healers.

Unlike Golondrina and the others, he does not conduct healing rituals for individuals outside of his family, but he will advise and direct those who come to him on the preparation and use of medicinal plants. While the other healers vary in their methods of healing, how they think about plants links them together. For them, plants are more than substances with curative properties; plants have a metaphysical aspect to them as well. The use of plants to cure illnesses caused by use of magic is common to many cultures. My consultants describe plants (and other ritual objects) as possessing *poder*, meaning power or will. They are also thought to have a spirit, not in the sense of a soul but more akin to energy. It is because of this power and energy that plants, especially those with known curative properties and a strong smell or taste, are effective in alleviating mental or emotionally based illnesses. This is in keeping with Trotter and Chavira's description of niveles, which was discussed earlier.

Rue is an especially strong plant. The smoke from its leaves can be used to cure earaches. The stems and leaves of the plants are sometimes used in a *barrida* to heal someone who might be a victim of witchcraft. This plant is one of Mr. Madrigal's best sellers. The person affected is ritually swept with a bundle of fresh rue while prayers are recited over him or her. Rue can also be used to magically cause someone harm. When I asked Mr. Madrigal how, he explained that some plants are variable depending on the intent of each user. Further, he believes that the character of a person determines the smell he or she will associate with rue. If a person is of good character and intentions, the plant will have an agreeable aroma; someone who is of bad character will find the plant has a noxious smell.

Golondrina is of the same mind, equating pleasant-smelling plants with positive results. Pleasant smells are thought to draw helpful spiritual entities and to ward off those of evil intent. Rue, she believes, is an especially powerful plant. Both Golondrina and Mr. Madrigal feel that the plant has great sensitivity; if part of a plant is taken for purposes of witchcraft, the remainder will wither and die.

Rosemary and basil are plants that are not variable. Their aromatic stems and leaves are used in *barridas* to cure insomnia. Having some in your home or on your person is thought to bring good luck. As a tea they are used for insomnia and nervousness. These plants are believed to contain only positive energy.

Epazote is a strong-smelling, foul-tasting herb used to rid the body of intestinal worms when ingested as a tea. Golondrina uses this plant in *humosas* (burned as incense) or in a barrida to cure a person of what she calls larvas mentales (mental worms.) She believes, as Mr. Madrigal does, that what affects the physical body affects the spiritual body in a like fashion. Both healers were asked why smell is such an important indicator of a plant's efficaciousness. Mr. Madrigal believes that it is the spirit of the plant we are encountering when we take in its aroma. Golondrina feels that it is through our sense of smell that we test whatever we encounter before bringing it into our bodies, especially what cannot be seen.

Mr. Madrigal and the other healers hold a special place in a hierarchy of knowledge concerning plant use and belief. Their status is gained through study and perceived effectiveness by the community. They are highly specialized and have in place a philosophy of healing based on tradition and personal experience.

"*La planta es la vida,*" Mr. Madrigal said to me one day, emphasizing that plants are not just a metaphor for life but also for how we think about life, giving evidence that a belief system that some might view as archaic or folkloric is very much at home in one of America's largest cities and is effectively meeting the needs of a large group of its citizens.

Toward a Regional Ethnobotany

It was difficult in some cases during this research to establish the exact species used, owing to conflicting botanical classifications and folk nomenclature. In the literature, in some instances, different varieties are grouped under the same genus name. There was also evidence of substitution, as in the case of *Altamisa* (*Artemisia franserioides*) and Wormwood (*Artemisia ludoviciana* Nutt.). Both are in the *Artemisia* family; but Altamisa can be difficult to obtain, since it grows primarily in high altitudes. Altamisa Mexicana (*Chrysanthymum ambrosioides*), which grows at lower elevations, can be substituted for the two plants.[5] Substitutions are important for suggesting how a curer's medicine kit can remain essentially the same, even as the person moves into a different environmental zone; or how the idea of a particular remedy can diffuse through different environmental zones. Substitutions are also part of the historical process. Certain indigenous plants are displaced by invasive species as well as by adoption of introduced plants through trade. In the next few pages I offer a taxonomy of the more commonly used healing plants that I encountered.

The red mescal bean, or Texas mountain laurel seed, is used as an amulet, often incorporated into a charm for the house or to carry in a purse or pocket; it is believed to ward off witches or bad energy. Other items thought to help the bearer are basil leaves, for luck and money; ajo macho (male garlic) is for spiritual protection.

When Cabeza de Vaca began his life among the Indians he noted certain plants being used as purgatives and commented on the harvest of pecans by the local Indians. They also ground mesquite beans to use as food and as a sweetener. At least once a semester a student tells me that he or she used to chew mesquite bean pods as a child. I did the same as a child. They can be chewed like gum or ground into a meal and used to sweeten corn meal or drinks. The leaves also can be boiled; the water is strained and used as an eyewash.[6]

Nogal (pecan) is used among Mexican Americans for ringworm and as a disinfectant in the treatment of wounds and sores. Mr. Madrigal believes it strengthens the blood and he drinks it as a tea brewed from the leaves. There are botanical substances that to me seem uniquely Texan, but in truth they are part of the continuing interaction between people and plants across Mexico and the borderlands.

Nopal (cactus) is one of those items. Every spring on Saturdays or maybe Sundays when I was a girl, my family would go for a drive outside of the city. We lived in Corpus Christi at the time. This was the time during Lent when the young cactus pads were in abundance. My parents and grandmother would harvest the cactus while we played in the car or somewhere near them. Many other families also took part, and the days became social events with the same families harvesting along the fence lines on a regular basis. During the week when I stayed with my grandmother I would help pull out the tiny thorns that lay embedded in the palms of her hands. She cooked the cactus with eggs and chiles, or she served it marinated as a cold salad. We stopped harvesting in this manner years ago, but cactus is now so popular here that it can be purchased in the vegetable section of supermarkets. Although it is still considered primarily a Lenten food, many restaurants serve it on a year-round basis. Half a cup of *nopal* eaten in the morning is also believed to help keep blood sugar in check.

Chamomile, *manzanilla*, is one of the most popular plants among Mexican Americans. Its use is varied. Some of its applications are for nausea, insomnia, head colds, nervousness, and cramps. It is taken as a tea. Mr. Madrigal will sometimes use it in barridas to sweep sleeplessness away from his wife.

Cedar (*Juniperus ashei* Buchh.) is used at the beginning of some ceremonies, especially when a large gathering is present or expected. Small amounts of cedar are placed on hot coals and the smoke is fanned to the different corners of the room, or a person is bathed in its smoke. In cases of susto, the person is treated by being brushed with plants; cedar is one commonly used. Aside from knowing the curative properties of plants, another consideration is the relationship between the plant and healer.

How one relates to plants is important in their efficacy. Mr. Madrigal related an incident that involved an angry plant. He believes that plants know their owners and that they can react at times with human responses. He was trimming back *yerba buena* (spearmint) one day, but instead of taking it for use as medicine, he threw it away in a garbage can. The mistake, he believes, was in throwing away the cuttings in view of the remaining plants. Since then, the mint will not grow in that area. They withdrew their favor. He and others have told me that rue will grow only for its owner. It recognizes the touch of the person and will die if cut by anyone else. This was explained to me by Mr. Madrigal in logical terms: a person has a particular feel to them, a vibration that is solely their own. The plant recognizes this and reacts accordingly.

In my gathering of plants I was instructed by Golondrina to give a mental directive to the plant I was going to use for healing as I picked it, telling the plant its purpose and on whose behalf this curing was to take place. The point is for the healer's energy to work with the energy of the plant in the process. This goes to the idea of all things intrinsically holding power and also that we are all connected to the world around us. By asking elements of the natural world to assist in healing we are reaffirming our connection to it and incorporating the individual being healed back into it.

For Mr. Madrigal and the others, plants are sentient beings with something akin to a mind. Plants of great efficacy are generally considered more sensitive. This is why Mr. Madrigal believes that rue, rosemary, and mountain laurel are so hard to propagate. These particular plants are difficult to grow at first but once established are rather hardy. He sees the difficulty as evidence of their capabilities and therefore more worthy of an effort than other plants.

The healing plant is a fixture in cultures globally. In studying plants through a cultural lens we begin to understand how much of what we think and our manner of behavior is tied to the natural world. As a researcher, how people think about the natural world gives me insight into the structure of their world and their place in it. For the healers, plants are symbols of power that can be used for helping or hindering a person. Because the same plant can be used in a spiritual or organic fashion, in a good or evil way, it speaks to the duality many of the healers believe define us as human beings.

Healing with plants is a timeless tradition among Native and Mestizo peoples; it is but one aspect of the complex modalities available to healers as they engage their communities. In the next chapter I discuss how the nature of the curandersimo is changing yet again to meet the needs of changing communities.

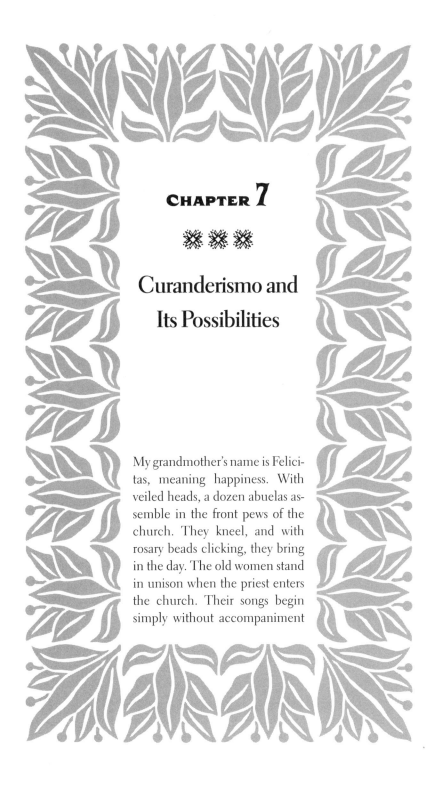

CHAPTER 7

✳ ✳ ✳

Curanderismo and Its Possibilities

My grandmother's name is Felici-
tas, meaning happiness. With
veiled heads, a dozen abuelas as-
semble in the front pews of the
church. They kneel, and with
rosary beads clicking, they bring
in the day. The old women stand
in unison when the priest enters
the church. Their songs begin
simply without accompaniment

and they raise their reedy voices to God, thanking Him for the new morning. They sing to God the songs brought with them from Mexico; songs of saints and the Blessed Mother, of sin and redemption; songs that crossed the border many years ago — or that were here before there was a border. The priest enters, tiny bells sound, and we all stand. With his back to his people, the priest chants the opening benediction in Latin. I am alone in the rear of the church, a small brown girl just able to see over the top of the pew in front of her. The smell of wax and copal wrap around me as I watch my dad. He attends the priest, serving in turn as an altar boy, an usher, and a collector of tithes. He moves quickly and quietly, shifting from one duty to the other. My eyes follow him through the church as he passes the Stations of the Cross, following the footsteps of Jesus without even knowing it.

Few people come to this service; it starts at six in the morning. Usually it is the devoted and the very old. I am the exception. I stay with my grandmother most evenings; my father takes us to mass in the morning and then we go home. There we pick up my younger sister and brother (still an infant) and go to a daycare center run by Carmelite nuns. It is a cold place run by light-colored women who cane the Spanish off my skin; learning English is the only way to get them to stop.

However, for now, this precious hour of worship belongs to my father, grandmother, and me. I love the old women and their songs. They belong to a sect devoted to the worship of the Virgen de Guadalupe. In a cluster, they exit the sanctuary, and I listen to their greetings for one another, the hugs, and the kisses on the cheek. They see me, and I am included in their number for an instance. "*Ah, Lisa, venites con tu abuela?*" (you came with your grandmother?), "*te pareces mas y mas a tu apá*" (you favor your father more and more). My father receives praise for bringing me to church. He stands just inside a small closet in the foyer, selling votive candles to those leaving prayers and petitions at the feet of the saints housed in the church. A naked light bulb hangs suspended above him, casting shadows on rows of potential miracles.

There are two small chapels on either end of the foyer; these are where most of the candles end up. Their glow touches my skin as I walk near. I explore the chapels while waiting for my elders. They are cave-like; the outside light cannot compete with the shadows thrown up against the walls by the hundreds of tiny candles. It is always twilight in here. The hypnotic dance of the candlelight draws me in, while the wrought iron grating of the *candelarias* steadies me as I stare at the tiny photos of people long gone. Dozens of pictures, faded flowers, and scribbled notes are pinned or laid beneath the statues, *promesas* made and kept. All about me are the whispered prayers, hopes, and desires of the poor. My father calls me as he locks the closet and we exit through the heavy oak doors into the hazy morning, the dew covers my arms softly; the morning rises to greet us.

Seeing the world this way, through a child's eyes, is how I try to live my life. I approach the work I do with healers and yerberos the same way. My time with them is filled with wonderment and a youngster's curiosity but I never can I forget why I am here; I have colleagues to remind me and books to chastise my involvement.

Coming Full Circle

The history of the Southwest is one of mythologizing Native people and subsuming the Mexicans. Politically and socially, Mexicanos are part of the landscape in a manner that is constantly being redefined. In David Montejano and Arnoldo de Leon's revisionist histories we see how Mexican and Mexican American populations at different times are categorized as Spanish, Indian, Mexican, Caucasian, Hispanic, Latin, White, and Brown.[1] The terms and their meanings are in constant flux, both how they are applied to people and how people perceive themselves.

In the mid-twentieth century, efforts in self-determination quickened. We see this in South Texas with the formation of LULAC, the GI Forum, and labor movements. The Kennedys' (John and Robert) acknowledgment of Mexican Americans political viability and Lyndon Johnson's "War on Poverty" acted in concert to move Mexican Americans onto the national landscape. The Chicano Movement of the late 1960s and 1970s gave Mexican American youth an origin myth, Aztlán, and a cohesive cultural identity as mestizos along with various icons, low riders, *vato locos*, and farm workers. In the anthropological literature of those years, voices emerged that serve as a foundation for many of us in the work of Octavio Roman and Américo Paredes.

Health care among Mexican Americans is an area that began to receive attention during this time. Government sponsored studies were conducted to assess the current state and needs of Mexican American communities.[2] Health studies and others that addressed social services used background material that in some cases perpetuated stereotypes of Mexicanos as superstitious and nature dominated.[3] Those studies include references to curanderismo and its practice in mostly rural areas. Curanderismo in academic writing of the 1960s was depicted as a cultural relic that would disappear when Mexican Americans assimilated into the larger American culture.[4] In fact, there was little mention of curanderismo as a practice in urban areas, which perpetuated the stereotype of Mexicanos as rural or unsophisticated. The scholars conducting early work in curanderismo did not approach it as a complex, philosophically rich tradition but as a lack of access to modern medicine, modern thinking, and a perceived reaction to a fatalistic view of the world. These are viewpoints shaped by a lack of understanding of the Mexican American population in the borderlands and their long history of colonization.

This is what I found when I began my work. I believed that the work in curanderismo was narrow in its scope, long hijacked by convenient and outdated explanations. Not totally on their own (historians are also to blame), but in some measure, the early ethnographers of the southwestern United States laid a foundation for a Euro-centric view of the inhabitants that has persisted. Undoing the stereotypes and outdated explanations is best accomplished in the discipline that gave birth to them. Anthropology has taught me to ask questions that can only be answered in a holistic fashion. Asking the question, "Why is this plant used?" begins a discussion of its use as medicine but leads to discussion on the spiritual energy it holds and to a difference between domestic varieties versus wild.

This is the way the discipline was intended in practice. At the heart of anthropology is the idea to look at the connections. We have forgotten this in trying to divorce anthropology from its own history, in carving out subdisciplines unrelated in training to one another beyond the teaching of first-year fundamentals. Because of anthropology, I can understand the historical and cultural process of who and what I am and those of my people in a way that the disciplines of history, psychology, or any of the natural sciences can not ever offer. This understanding, though, is heightened because the training I received came from cultural anthropologists as well as an archeaologist/ethnobotanist and a medical anthropologist. The interplay between these areas allows me to engage a fuller examination of healers and their work.

Healing the Border

In the course of this study, I have learned that the worldview that guides curanderismo also guides the work of many scholars, artists, and activists in this area; often these occupations overlap for individuals. In keeping with the fluid nature of borderland identity, people occupy multiple spaces of "being in the world." Nothing better exemplifies this than the work by Chicana feminists and writers, who have long dealt with issues of border conflict and its many incarnations. One of these incarnations is *la mestiza*.[5] It is an identity born of conflict, as Gloria Anzaldúa writes, "Within us and within *la cultura chicana*, commonly held beliefs of the white culture attack commonly held beliefs of the Mexican culture, and both attack commonly held beliefs of the indigenous culture."[6] Anzaldúa's *Borderlands, La Frontera*, published in 1987, introduced a method of examining the self in a reflexive political and social dimension. Sonia Saldívar-Hull writes that as a treatise that is "above all a feminist one," it opens up a radical way of restructuring the way we study history. Using a new genre she calls *autohistoria*, Anzaldúa presents history as a serpentine cycle rather than a linear narrative.[7]

Anzaldúa boldly defined herself as a person of the border, one who cannot deny the conqueror or conquered within her. Anzaldúa's work did not emerge from a vacuum but developed from the political presence of Chicanas active but largely ignored in *el movimieno* of the 1970s.[8] The innovation of *Borderlands* was in defining a spirituality that spoke to the mestiza nature of Chicana feminism. Anzaldúa uses Aztec religious icons to forge a new spiritual/political identity, Coatlicue, the serpent goddess and mother of all gods. In Coatlicue she presents the other face of the Virgen de Guadalupe, the indigenous one. She uses this image to refute Spanish erasure of native religion and revises the male-centered telling of Chicano history.[9]

As much as Anzaldúa's work has defined and influenced the subsequent work of Chicana scholars and writers, it is still largely dependent on the origin myths of the Aztecs as the ancestors of Mexican Americans. But there are writers and academics who are transgressing that icon by weaving in their own sense of indigineity, such as Rudolfo Anaya, Pat Mora, and Carmen Tafolla, to name a few. It is an area ripe for investigation. My own early work began as a comparison between Comanche medicine tradition and curanderismo.[10] I believe that through a closer look at the meaning and role of spirituality in a comparative framework we can construct an avenue in understanding the connections between our mestizaje and present-day indigenous cultures. The work of establishing these connections is visible in the efforts by Chicana writers and academics who are examining indigenous religious icons as centers of resistance and power, such as the work by Partrisia Gonzales, who is profiled in this chapter.

Chicanas and other Latinas began in the 1990s to expand their work in the area of spirituality. Jeanette Rodríguez's book, *Our Lady of Guadalupe*, fashions the image of the Virgen de Guadalupe as an empowering image in religious and secular spheres. For Rodriguez, "Guadalupe is of God," and thus provides a positive symbol of mestizaje.[11] In essence, Rodriguez is saying that God is mestizo or mestiza and thus creates a powerful, salient image for women who are twice marginalized in the United States, once for being Mexican and again for being female. Rodriguez's book is an important one in the area of mestizo theology as expressed by Virgilio Elizondo and others within the Catholic Church.[12] The outcome is double-edged. On the one hand, it brings recognition and legitimacy to one of the Church's largest and most devout populations, the varied people resulting from the Spanish conquest. But it also is a movement of cultural appropriation. The Catholic Church through history actively and often forcefully erased the indigenous identity and cultural practices of its converts and members. It is prudent for the Church at this time to take a stance of tolerance and inclusiveness, in the face of shrinking membership and a political atmosphere of increasing multiculturalism.

Whether it is the image of the Virgen, Tonantzín, or Coatlicue, the move towards creating a Chicana Feminist Spirituality is an effort to gain and affirm voice by exerting a historical and continuing presence through our indigenous roots and religions, thereby destabilizing notions of the Mexicana as an intruder, or worse, as a voiceless aspect of the landscape.

In My Own Way

Several of the healers told me that I have the don for healing but they also intimated that this don is not to practice the way they do (though I was assured it is possible for me to heal people). My *don* manifests itself in the work I produce. Golondrina and the sisters believe that recounting their stories and keeping traditions alive through my writing and teaching is my calling; this is my healing. I have described my research and writing to the people who work with me as purposeful, a happy obligation, my contribution to the community and to culture. I am perfectly cognizant of my role as an educator and a role model for my students, with whom I often share a similar background. In this sense I belong to the community in the same way as the healers.

I bring to the tradition of curanderismo my own intellectual agenda, one that is influenced by scholars and writers from various backgrounds, not just anthropology. I believe this approach is in keeping with the syncretic nature of the tradition, and in turn this highlights areas for study not previously considered. Anthropology is also syncretic and the discipline allows me the latitude to experiment and question without reservation.

Recently I gave a lecture at the University of Texas Health Science Center. It was for a Latina/o medical student organization and was attended by group of seventy five to one hundred people. Mr. Madrigal came with me and I started the talk with a story about my grandmother and father. They had an encounter with the devil once on a lonely stretch of highway between Corpus Christi and Laredo back in the early 1960s. After telling the story I mentioned that I once told this same story in a class as an undergraduate at the urging of a professor. At that time a fellow classmate asked if I believed my grandmother's account of what happened. I was struck for a moment; I had never considered not believing her. I responded, "What was I supposed to tell her? 'Grandma, are you full of crap?' Of course I believed her, she's my grandmother."

The audience broke out in laughter, as I had expected they would. Once their laughter subsided I told them the point I was trying to make concerned worldview. My grandmother lived in a world where the living, dead, supernatural, technological, and natural realms could all occupy the same space at the same time, like an interconsciousness of space and location. This is what I grew up with, so of course I believed her. They, as doctors working in South Texas, will also have patients who think in this fashion. It might not be articulated, but it exists at our most fundamental level, the subconscious. If they approach clients with the understanding that there is more than one way to see the world, meaningful dialogue can take place and they can be more effective in their job. By laying this idea down at the beginning of my talk, things went smoothly. Mr. Madrigal then gave a presentation on plants, and we passed around specimens so people could see, smell, and hear about the materials common to this area. Ten or fifteen years ago our appearance at such a gathering would have been unthinkable.

The talk drew a positive response and an invitation for next year, as well as the possibility of holding a small seminar in the near future. This is in contrast to the first time I gave a lecture to a group of medical interns. They were overall negative and not accepting of what one called "New Age pop psychology." What I learned between that first time and this latest talk reflects my own growing awareness of my position as a person who traverses cultures, a negotiator in much the same way as the curanderas. I shifted my position and thought—in what manner would a traditional western thinker approach this? The answer was to leave the metaphysics out at the beginning. By explaining worldview as something we all adhere to in some manner, the rest of the talk, including the supernatural aspects, makes sense because it is contextual. In the next section I introduce contemporary Chicana academics whose work in the area of indigenous healing I find relevant.

Pati Gonzales

Patrisia Gonzales is a journalist who, with Roberto Rodriguez, her husband, writes "The Column of the Americas." It is syndicated in newspapers
across the country and on the Internet. Their columns are commentaries
on political actions (or inaction, as the case may be) on the part of gov-
ernments across North and South America. They also write about social
issues concerning Mexican Americans and indigenous groups. For Patrisia
and Roberto, Mexicans and Mexican Americans are indigenous peoples.
Patrisia's first-person articles are often a mixture of present-day events and
folkloric elements. Like Cruz Ortiz, the artist mentioned at the beginning
of this book, Patrisia weaves the two into a narrative tapestry that commu-
nicates on multiple levels to her readers. The following is from a column,
"Pot of Tears":

> The pot is telling. So I listen to its hum; throw a pot for tears welling,
> *las lloronas*; the women are weeping inside. Among my people, la
> llorona legends tell of the weeping woman who drowned her children
> when the Spaniards came. Perhaps presaging the Europeans' arrival,
> Moctezuma's sister went wailing in the streets, "My children, we are
> lost." La llorona tells us something is wrong with society, that there
> are many forms of madness — like Andrea Yates' [a Texas mother who
> killed her five children in June 2001] or the mama who lighted Christ-
> mas lights all year for the son who never came back from 'Nam.
>   Not all lloronas kill their children. They wander among bodies
> of water, like spirits, for water is cold like death and flows like emo-
> tions. They provoke us into right action, as fear of death often does.
> Some do not cry, but rather cry out for justice, for the disappeared of
> the continent's dirty wars, for sweatshop workers; some call us from
> the spirit world, like the missing and murdered women in Juarez,
> Mexico. Others march, and scold society and politicians.[13]

La llorona (the weeping woman) is a character from a cautionary tale.[14]
As children, when misbehaving or unwilling to observe bedtime, we were
corrected and silenced with the phrase, "Behave or la llorona will get you."
Patrisia uses la llorona and the elements associated with her — water, sor-
row, and death — to move society towards acknowledging and accepting the
responsibilities of injustices and violence perpetuated on women.

Patrisia practices healing with words as well as with oils, herbs, and
flowers, and in her work she focuses on personal, emotional anguish that
can haunt a person. Patrisia believes that words are medicine; they have

the power to heal. She was raped years ago and found that she did not have a way to articulate the experience; the violence had taken away her use of language. Gradually she found her voice again. She now conducts workshops to teach other women how to use language and how to write to bring trauma out of the body. The writing workshops combine journaling, meditation, recognition of the four elements of the natural world as sources for healing, and Buddhist and indigenous thought. Participants often cry openly when bringing to surface difficult memories. She says, "The power of words can make people cry, purifying their spirit and heart and their body. Prayers are the words that release the harm from our body. We've been taught to pray in silence, and we need to learn to pray out loud again. The physical experience of crying cannot be separated from the spiritual emotional aspect of body."[15] Patrisia is affirming that the physical being cannot be separated from experience.

Patrisia studies with a Kickapoo elder in San Antonio and has also received training from Mexican and Nahua healers. She has also shown an interest in working with two of my main consultants, Golondrina and Jacinto. Because Patrisia sees Mexican Americans as indigenous, she does not call her practice curanderismo. To her the term is tied closely with Spanish colonialism. Her varied approach in healing is in keeping with the tradition's plasticity towards integration of outside methods and techniques. She is adding to it by bringing in knowledge from other areas of spirituality, including Reiki. My consultants see her as a curandera and she acknowledges that what troubles her most with the term is that people too often associate it with *brujeria* or witchcraft.

Yolanda Leyva

Yolanda Leyva, historian and curandera, sees her work as a way to heal historical trauma. Through Yolanda's introduction I have become part of a network of women in whose company can be found local political and community activists, educators, writers, and artists. Yolanda took a position at the University of Texas at El Paso in the fall of 2001; there she is concentrating on border history and developing a museum on border immigration. She writes,

> Living back on the border, where the divisions are so great and painful and the people so resilient and persistent, I knew would be exciting and challenging. Returning to the place where I could say, in the most profound way, 'I am who I am because I have been there . . .'

meant that I would be confronting an often painful history, my own and that of my people in a myriad of ways, on a daily basis. It meant that, for my own survival, I had to continue my efforts to make sense of the painful stories and to find ways to create a healing history.[16]

Yolanda practices curanderismo and uses the healing nature of the tradition to examine history and to bring into the discussion factors that have led to the disenfranchisement of individuals along the border area. She is illuminating the historiography of scholars like Emma Pérez, Vicki Ruiz, and Alexandra Minna Stern, with an approach by Eduardo Duran and Bonnie Duran, who believe that "The practice of psychology must be historicized. They urge their colleagues to understand the history behind the pain. Only by understanding history will psychologists be able to effectively work with Native Americans and other colonized peoples."[17] But the healing of those wounds are not for everyone, as Patrisia Gonzales notes when she writes, "And why is it some of us, but not all, assume the burden strap and carry the grief for our peoples' sufferings?"[18]

By acknowledging the trauma inflicted on individuals during the process of colonization, a process that continues today in many ways, we can begin to heal ourselves. Yolanda argues that this is not promoting a "history of victimization." Edén Torres writes, "If we understand that oppression is not simply about political or institutional discrimination but that it is also a form of mental, physical, spiritual, and emotional abuse, we can cleanse oursleves and stop internalizing the hatred and humiliation we experience." [19] Indeed, curanderismo pushes an individual to take ownership of her or his illness, signifying that the cure is primarily through the efforts of the individual and not an outside agency. Everything that is needed for an individual to be healed, she or he already possesses. It is role of a curandera or curandero to guide the individual to a state of wholeness. By using curanderismo in her scholarly work and in teaching, Yolanda and other women are expanding the possibilities where indigenous methodologies and philosophies can be applied.

Vangie

Vangie is an occupational and speech therapist who works with babies and infants with special needs. Recently she finished her training and practicum to become a registered massage therapist. When asked if she considers herself a curandera, the answer is "not yet;" she feels that ultimately she will become one. For her the act of becoming a curandera is more purposeful and developmental than that of the healers I consulted with for this book. In part, taking on the role of a curandera for Vangi is, by her own admission, "a way of going back to the curanderos of my mother and father, using estafiate, vinegar, and the other things which were a part of my growing up."[20] During our conversation, Vangi told me that this movement towards a massage practice came after the death of her mother, but she did not indicate any type of divine intercession as the healers have described. She was very close to her mother; understandably, her passing had an impact on Vangi's life. She considers her decision to become a *sobadora* (masseuse) "deliberate" and "planned." She feels she will take on the role later in life.

The question becomes who can lay claim to being called a curandera or curandero? The deliberate approach taken by Vangi is to ask if it is analogous to the spiritual awakening experienced by the healers. Will the plasticity of the tradition allow for a redefining of the base parameters, recognizing who becomes a healer or who is a healer? These are unanswerable questions. I believe the answer lies in part, on whether the community acknowledges the person as a curandera/o. The tradition revolves around community, not the individual. The recognition of a curandera/os' don begins with the healer, but community acknowledgement is necessary for the individual to claim status.

Conchita's Story

If curanderismo has a future, it is of a different face than the one my grandmothers were used to seeing, the one I saw as a girl. Its future exists in people like Conchita, Golondrina's daughter. At the early age of sixteen, she is actively exploring her world through electronic media and in the classroom. She recently began studying Buddhism and meditates every morning before going to school. Will she weave threads of this religion into her practice? All indications are that she will. Curanderismo is a *mezcla* of approaches and concepts. Conchita will bring to the practice ideas that are informed by her world and her experiences. In this fashion, she is in keeping with our mestizo ancestry that gave birth to curanderismo all those centuries ago.

When I started working with Golondrina, Conchita was in the second grade. I have watched her grow up, a skinny, tiny girl, and quiet, but always curious. She was at times like a street urchin — wise beyond her years, wily, taking advantage of any given situation, and always fiercely loyal to her mom. At an early age she was putting into practice what she had observed and learned from her mother. Once, when we were driving to her home after a visit to mine, I gave a heavy sigh. Without missing a beat she told me, "You're worried about something. You need to pray on it and listen to your internal Christ." She was ten at the time; by the time she was thirteen, she had conducted her first healing ritual. She readily interprets her own dreams as well as those of her mother. She keenly observes the world around her and applies an interpretation to people and events in a fashion that is neither empirical nor metaphysical alone, but increasingly a combination of the two.

Like all teenagers, she is dealing with the usual — school, relationships, and tests for college entrance. Her taste in music is mainstream but with an edge. She reads science fiction and magical fantasy literature. She is interested in all things Goth and prefers black nail polish to red. Rarely do I find her not wearing her headphones. Her mom indulges her hunger for CDs and books. Conchita would rather spend an afternoon or evening in a bookstore than in front of the television, but talking on the phone is her vice.

Occasionally I am asked to mediate an argument between Golondrina and her daughter. How many anthropologists can claim this experience? Lately it has been about freedom. Conchita wants to be on her own more; "My mom doesn't understand." Golondrina wants to keep her close. I do not take sides but draw on my own memories of being a teenager and of my mom's frustrations with me — when I give advice.

Conchita's life is like that of thousands of other teenagers, the quintessential American teenage experience of exploration, growth of individuality, and increasing independence from one's parents. She is different in that she is learning and practicing healing techniques that are timeless. She wants to be a psychologist when she grows up, and I tease her about becoming the first licensed curandera. In essence, I believe, she will be. Will she ever practice curanderismo the way her mother does? The way Lizzie or Jo Ann do? I do not know. She may give up that part of her life all together, but I argue that for her the intermingling is normal for her and others like her — children and grandchildren of healers. It is normal and will be present in their lives in some form or fashion for the whole of it. The mechanics of curanderismo is on the ground working everyday as seen in the manner that culture operates.

Healing Ourselves

In the changing educational, political and social face(s) of the Mexicana and Mexicano many things are possible. We seek to heal the individual as well as our communities. Curanderismo offers a model of how many of us feel the world operates. Imagine, that which we call our body is not really meaningful in and of itself; we are basically containers. Further, all around us is energy (power)—it has always been there and always will be. We are drawn to this energy and it gives us meaning. We can learn to manipulate it and make it purposeful, but always the connection to the energy outside of our bodies continues; it is this bond that makes us whole. Illness and troubles occur when there is a rupture in that connection. I propose that this philosophy of interconnectedness is one that guides the lives and actions of many of us who live in the borderlands.

Understanding these connections, I believe, is what motivates many of the Chicana and Chicano professors, artists, and community activists who work and live in San Antonio. There is so much healing needing to take place in this city and others like it across the Southwest. San Antonio has the highest teen pregnancy rate in the state. The majority of young mothers are Latinas, some as young as thirteen. We have one of the, if not the, highest dropout rate(s) in the state. There are multiple generations of families who make the Courts, public assistance housing, their home. This is the San Antonio that tourists do not see, but this is the San Antonio who makes their beds, serves their tables, cleans their toilets, and adds that Latin flair the Chamber of Commerce likes to promote.

This is the background from where many of my colleagues and I came. These are the memories that motivate us to try and implement changes. We know that we are the lucky ones; that because of our intellect, talent, timing, and support we are traversing boundaries. We do it each in our own way; two people come to mind. One is Adán Hernández and the other Selena Catalá.

Adán is an artist whose work now hangs at the National Gallery in Washington D.C. He still lives in a working-class barrio. He regularly lectures at public schools about his art and what motivates him to paint. Adán believes that children need to see what people are capable of doing if they believe in themselves. He came and spoke to my class recently. His talk included a slide presentation of his art but also included why he works with young people. He told my students that we have an obligation to better our community. Selena runs an after-school program for young girls, the Escuelitas program. Escuelitas is part of Hispanas Unidas, a professional organization that brings together Latina activists of varied backgrounds. Escuelitas is a pregnancy intervention program that aids in building the girls' positive self-image, bringing in artists, writers and speakers from the community so the girls intellectual experiences are broadened; they also work with a mentor on a one-to-one basis to improve their math and verbal skills. The mentors are college students who volunteer a semester at a time. Selena believes this relationship is important; the mentors are all Latinas or Latinos, and the girls get the message that college is possible. Selena always calls the girls "young ladies." She expects from them full participation and to be well behaved at all times. Her program is an option for the community service component in some of my classes. Students who participate in this program react with surprise at the lives of some of the girls; some find it familiar; none have ever backed off from continuing once they have started. I have one student who has participated for several years.

Selena and Adán are just two examples of the type of community involvement I have found to be vehicles for doing work that matters, for doing healing work. The healers have explained to me that anyone can heal; it is a matter of understanding that the ability exists and that the person is willing to learn how to use the energy in and around her or him to affect a change. In this way, we can see that healing is also a metaphor for social action and change. But we have to learn how to heal, how to implement change. This is what I have discovered in my return home: because of anthropology, I can use my training to communicate the needs of my community effectively. I also understand now why the Chicana feminists stress that our lives are political. Politics, after all, are about relationships; in the worldview of the borderlander, all things are connected. People like Adán, Selena, and myself, who occupy multiple worlds, are constructing a road for the generations of borderlanders to follow. As an indigenous person my world is one of interconnections and holism. Everything around me is connected to everything else; my mind and my heart are not two separate entities working together but two essences contained in the same flask. It is a timeless philosophy in an age that sees time as a precious commodity.

But I live and function in a world dominated by a European-based culture that dictates the separateness of the individual from her or his world and from those around her or him. It subscribes to a medical ethos that looks at illness separately from the physical and spiritual body, treating the illness without *listening* to the person. It values the written word, not the spoken, and it seeks to conquer the land, not appreciate it for the living thing that it is. I asked rhetorically in an earlier chapter whether I could prove myself a good anthropologist without selling myself out. Can I gain success and scholarship and yet not lose sight of why I wanted to return to South Texas? I do not know the answer. I have to trust that if I live right today, tomorrow will take care of itself. This is what I have relearned in the course of learning from the healers: the present is what we need to work on in order for tomorrow to fall into place.

EPILOGUE

ON FEBRUARY 14, 1995, I received a letter of acceptance from the anthropology department at the University of Michigan. I cried. It had taken me over five years to complete the eighty hours of course work necessary to receive my Bachelor of Arts degree. I was thirty-six years old and working as a customer accounts representative with AT&T, as was my husband. The company ran on a top-down hierarchy in a constant reactive mode, dependent on market competition. As a "rep," my well being and that of my co-workers was at the whim of first-line managers whose order of business was job security — their own. We were supposed to work as a unit, several of us grouped together under the guidance of a team leader. The relationship, actually, was often acrimonious, as with one manager whom we all just called "Ochoa." I remember him smugly telling us our civil rights ended when we walked through the company door.

Our monthly evaluations were based not just on how we treated the customer (our calls were frequently monitored), but also on how frequently we delivered "excellent" customer service and how much revenue we generated for the company during each contact. It was a repetitious, highly stressful job, but it paid good money. The constant emphasis on the bottom line definitely took its toll on each rep. Some mornings I would find tiny crescent moon-shaped indentations in the palm of my hands where I had pressed my fingernails into my flesh while asleep. The stress had to find a way out and it did so during the night. By 1995, I had logged nearly fifteen years with the company.

I never had any real intent of leaving AT&T to pursue an advanced degree when I returned to school. My BA was something I needed to finish, left pending from my adolescence. AT&T paid for classes in certain subjects but others, like those in anthropology, came out of my own pocket. Anthropology did not fit into the company's scheme of "useful" subjects. I took classes whenever possible, in some semesters only one, in other semesters as many as three. There were days that started for me at four in the morning. My work schedule ran from six in the morning to two-thirty in the afternoon. Occasionally on these long days I fell asleep at the university library while waiting for an evening class to start. Finally, in my last year of studies, I took a leave of absence from my job. Johnny was out of work with a psychological disability. Later he was diagnosed with PTSD (Post Traumatic Stress Disorder) resulting from his tour in Vietnam. Whether the heavy authoritative hierarchy we worked under aggravated his condition, we will never know. By 1994, he was in a deep depression and was not able to function properly at his job. We lived off my student loans and his income from company disability payments.

At this point in my life, I was an honors student working on a thesis based on research conducted during the previous summer, my first work with Golondrina. Ironically, while I was an excellent student, at work I was not considered a good "corporate player." My employee evaluations, while not dismal, were certainly never stellar; my revenue numbers were frequently the lowest of my team. I was told that I would never make manager. I think back to my life as a corporate employee and cannot remember enjoying any of the fifteen years I spent at AT&T.

I found my niche in the study of anthropology. My undergraduate advisor suggested graduate school and eventually doctoral studies. When my acceptance letter from the University of Michigan arrived, I knew that my life would never be the same. A little later in the spring, I received word from the National Science Foundation with the news of a three-year fellowship. Before hearing from the NSF, Johnny and I talked and decided that Michigan was the school I should accept. They offered the most in terms of academics, funding, and benefits. On the strength of a letter, we decided to sell our house, one of our vehicles, and almost all of our furniture. We left behind his children, our families, and our jobs. Our family and friends said we were crazy.

The day came to turn in my resignation and identification badge. It was an important day in my adult life. I am at the tail end of a generation that believes a person works for a corporation like AT&T for life. As much as I hated the job, it afforded me an enviable security. I never doubted my decision, but I felt a nagging sense of anxiety. In the end, my resignation was very anticlimactic; there was an exit interview and papers to sign, and that was that. As I passed through a large open area, ringed by cubicles where managers hid away from the wage labor, I said goodbye to several women (now ex-coworkers) who were staffing a row of computer screens. Tiny blips representing individual workstations blinked off and on as people logged in and out of the system — every on-line employee was accounted for by the minute. After several quick hugs and well wishes, I headed towards the door. Turning back, I waved farewell and loudly said, "Tell Ochoa he can kiss my brown ass good-bye because I'm never coming back!" The door slowly closed on a high volume of laughter, and I grinned at my own sassiness. My farewell exclamations were words many people often think about but will never say.

August 2002

I picked up the key for my office. The smell of paint was fresh; workmen were all around trying to get things ready for the new semester. My office was located in a brand-new building on the downtown campus, which sits on the perimeter of the San Antonio tourist area. I located my office and let myself in. The smell of newness greeted me at the door. No one had ever sat in my chair or used this keyboard. The walls were blank, the bookcases empty. In the coming year they would be filled with books in anthropology, Chicana feminism, poetry, Mexican American history, and books in ethnobotany. One shelf became an altar, and my grandmother's picture of *La Virgen de San Juan* was placed next to a family photo taken when my siblings and I were little. In the photo, my parents look toward the camera; they are beautiful, dressed in their best clothes, and their arms are filled with us, their children.

I sat in my standard office chair and looked out at the view of the city. In truth, it is not much of a view; I see the freeway to Laredo pointing the way to Mexico. Mr. Madrigal and I often take that road when we go to harvest plants. A parking lot, black top and hot, is across the street, and in the distance the spire of a Catholic church rises above the tree line. Still, my window faces the area of town that has given me an academic life. Just beyond the freeway and the pecan trees is Golondrina's house, a mere five miles down the road. Further west is Mr. Madrigal's home, and near him, the sisters. Collectively, these people are the reason I can look out this window today.

I sat and thought of my father and the rare few times I'd seen him cry — when I went off to college for the first time and when he was dying and memories of being a brown man in South Texas surfaced through the fog of pain killers. He spoke of having to swallow his pride at the indignations and hostilities aimed towards him. To my younger brother he said, *"gabachos*

te dejan con nada:" "white men will leave you with nothing." He always
keenly felt his own lack of education. I now realize that my journey has
been in part to honor him. "We all stand on someone's shoulders," is what
I tell my students; "we never travel alone." I said a short prayer of thanksgiving and cried a little for my father and Maggie, my sister-in-law, who did
not live long enough to see the end of this journey. I miss them dearly.

I pay the obligation I feel towards them, and others who wanted my success, in every class I teach and in the words I write. I consider my time with
students a blessing. To go from where I was as a child and in early adulthood to where I am today is testament to the poder that I saw, and continue
to see, in people like my family. I also see it in my students; many of them
have children, are married, or are returning to school as adults, just as I
did not too many years ago. I have students who follow the traditional track
of university life; they are young, living away from home for the first time,
exploring life and their new independence. Nevertheless, it is the nontradi-
tional older students, trying to do more than what society expects of them,
who truly hold my heart. When I talk with them or lecture in class, I apply
the lessons I have learned from my colleagues, gleaned from their writings
on Chicana\Chicano history, literature, and culture, to demonstrate that
we have the authority to say what our culture is and will become. What I
learned during those years of struggle I also pass on to them; if I can do it,
they can too. I tell them to go out and set the world on fire. There are other
lessons, too, learned in the course of fieldwork.

At my invitation, the curanderas — Golondrina, Lizzie, Jo Ann, Charlene, and Mr. Madrigal — came to my university and gave a talk. Approxi-
mately seventy people, mostly students, attended but there were also people
from the community. It was not a widely publicized talk and I was happy
with the number of people who came out for a weekday evening. I gave
a very short introduction of my part in the work and what I had learned
personally, saying in part what I stated at the beginning of chapter five, "I
know that many of you have come to see magic. We all want magic, but I
have to tell you there is no magic. This is the lesson I have learned from the
healers: What we call magic is faith, the miraculous — compassion. This is
what they use when working with their clients. This is what they want us to
learn. And with these two things, faith and compassion, we can cause the
incredible to happen; we can learn to heal ourselves."

I then introduced the panel, and each healer in turn talked about their
philosophy and practice. The audience asked questions about their beliefs,
source of power, and what to use for specific problems. At the end of the
talk, people lined up to ask their advice, to be spiritually healed, and to

just chat with them a bit. Several people thanked me for organizing the panel, saying that having the healers come and dialogue with a gathering was needed in the community. At first I felt uncomfortable not staying in control of the proceedings, but then I realized this type of interaction has always been one of my goals. I want people to understand curanderismo as something more than a way to cure cultural illnesses. As I listened to the healers talk about chakras, energy, gotu kola, love, and problems of the everyday, I knew that part of the gap was being closed. They were reaching out, demystifying the tradition. The audience responded enthusiastically. There was still that sense of wanting the incredible but the lessons are often difficult. People will always look for the easiest solution.

Two days later, Golondrina called to say that she enjoyed meeting Charlene and hearing her speak. "*Estamos en armonía* (we are in harmony)." She then said, "And you speak very well. I told Conchita, 'Liz finally got it, she understands.' You are very advanced and as your person changes, you will get better." The Ph.D. gives me the right to claim a certain space in academia but Golondrina's affirmation allows me to claim space as a healer.

I am a different person than I was when I received that letter from Michigan. Whether Michigan or the healers most shaped who I am today, I cannot say. But inkeeping with a borderlander's viewpoint, the journey forward will combine the two.

APPENDIX 1

Botanical Substances Used for Teas, Baths, Poultices, and Ritual Sweeping of the Body (Barrida)

BOTANICAL NAME	SPANISH	ENGLISH
Acacia smallii Isely	Huisache, Huizache	Huisache
Achillea lanulosa Nutt.	Real de oro	Yarrow
Agastache mexicanum ·	Toronjil	Giant Hyssop
Allium sativum L.	Ajo	Garlic
Aloe barbadensis Miller	Sávila, Zábila	Aloe Vera
Anemopsis californica Nutt.	Yerba del cancer (yerba mansa?)	
Artemisia franserioides	Altamisa	
Artemisia ludoviciana Nutt	Estafiate	Wormwood
Borago officinalis L.	Boraja	Borage
Buddleja perfoliata H.B.K.	Sueldao	Butterfly Bush
Capscium annum L.	Chile	Pepper (whole)
Castilleja indivisa Engelm.	Yerba del conejo	Indian paintbrush
Chenopodium ambrosioides L.	Epazote	Wormseed
Chrysanthemum ambrosioides	Altamisa Mexicana	feverfew
Cinnamomum zeylanicum Breyn	Canela	Cinnamon
Citrus aurantium L.	Limón verde	Lime
Cnidoscolus chayamansa McVaugh	Chaya	
Coriandrum sativum L.	Cilantro	Coriander
Cuminium cyminum L.	Comino	Cumin
Datura wrightii Regel	Tolvache; Toloache	Jimson Weed

BOTANICAL NAME	SPANISH	ENGLISH
Dichondria recurvata Tharp & Johnst.	Oreja del ratón	Pony foot
Eriobotrya japonica Lindl.	commonly referred to as Chinese plum	Loquat
Glandularia bipinnatifida	Verbena	Verbena
Goldenia canenscens	Oreja del raton	?
Haplopappus spinulosus (Pursh)	Árnica	Goldenweed
Hedeoma drummondii Benth.	Poleo Chino	Pennyroyal
Heterotheca latifolia Buckl.	Arnica, berro del monte	Camphor weed
Hieracium fendleri	Oreja de raton	?
Jatropha dioica Cerv.	Sangre de drago, sangre de grado	Leatherwood
Juglans spp.	Nogal	Pecan
Juniperus ashei Buchh.	Cedro	Cedar
Larrea tridentate (DC) Coville	Gobernadora	Creosote bush
Laurus nobilis	Laurel	Bay leaves
Leucophyllum frutescens Johnst.	Cenizo	Sage Brush
Magnolia grandiflora	Magnolia	Magnolia
Marrubium vulgare L.	Marrubio	Horehound
Matricaria recutita L.	Manzanilla	Chamomile
Medicago sativa L.	Alfalfa	Alfalfa
Mentha spicata L.	Yerba Buena	Mint
Ocimum basilicum L.	Albacar, Albahaca	Basil
Opuntia lindheimeri Engelm.	Nopal	Cactus
Oxalis dichodraefolia Gray	Raíz de la chata	Wood sorrel
Pavonia lasiopetala	Malva	Mallow
Perezia wrightii Gray	Árnica	Arnica
Persea americana Mill.	Avocate, Ahuacate	Avocado
Pimpinelle anisum L.	Anís	Anis
Piper auritum H.B.K.	Hoja Santa	Hoja Santa
Prosopis glandulosa Torr.	Mesquite	Mesquite
Quercus virginiana Mill.	Encino	Live Oak
Rhamnus catharticus L.	Cascara sagrada	Cascara sagrada
Rosmarinus officinalis L.	Romero	Rosemary
Ruta graveolens L.	Ruda	Rue
Salix nigra Marsh.	?	Willow
Sambucus mexicana Presl.	Sauco	Elderberry
Schinus molle L.	Pirul	Pepper Tree
Sophora secundiflora (Ortega) DC	Frijolillo	Texas Mountain Laurel
Tagetes lucida Cav.	Yerba Anís	Anis
Ungnadia speciosa Endl.	Ojo de Venado	Buckeye
Yucca constricta Buckl.	izote	Yucca
Zea mays L.	Barba de maíz	corn silk

APPENDIX 2

Ritual Material Used in Healing and Prayer

Any thing can be used as an item to heal or in black magic. The item is a type of amplifier working off the energy of the healer. However, the following items are most commonly used in curanderismo.

ITEM	USE
ajo macho	Spiritual protection
aloe vera	Cuts, burns; spiritual protection
alum (piedra de alumbre)	Curar susto
bath water	For client to use at home in ritual cure
bells/rattles	Push away bad spirits and reconfigure a person's aura
Bible	Kept on altar
cactus	Spiritual protection
candles	Prayers, healing, petitions: large or votive candles for prayers, column type for healing
chile	Limpias, humazos fresh or dried, dried for humazos. The hotter the pepper, the better
cloth/ handkerchief size	For bundling ritual material; to cover person being healed
deer antlers	Ceremonial use to ward off spirits
eggs	Evil eye, susto raw and in the shell for spiritual cleansings
feathers	Cleansings
flowers	Cleansings and baths
fruits	Cleansings passed over body or used in ritual cleansings of home

ITEM	USE
hands	For cleansing and healing passed over body or in a massage
incense	Draws sprits, carries prayers copal, myhrr, coffee, orange, cinnamon
mirrors	Reflecting light onto a person
mountain laurel bean	Spiritual protection, found in amulets
perfumes/oils	Spiritual cleansings
plants	See appendix 1
rosaries	Kept on altar or held by client
stones/crystals	When the task of healing is a particularly difficult one.
water	All types of healing

APPENDIX 3

Selected Prayers
Gathered during Fieldwork

Golondrina:

Prayer during ritual for susto/soul loss:

En el santo y bendito nombre del Señor, padre. En tu santo y bendito nombre del Señor, le pedimos a estos alimentos benditos de dios, que en tu santo y bendito nombre usa esta piedra bendita, perfumé bendito del Señor, quita el Señor, a mi hermana\hermano, todo lo que esta inutilizando su camino, su progreso, padre santísimo, por que grande es su poder, Señor y solo a ti reconocemos Señor padre santísimo en tu nombre le pedimos a esta piedra bendita que le retire a mi hermana, que le levante todo esto que le esta molestando, a su camino, a su vida, a su progreso a su atendimiento, en el santo bendito nombre del Señor, en tu santo bendito nombre, . . . (Lord's prayer) . . . Que tenga buena voluntad, que sigua a la luz. Tue que eres un niño de gran amor, que sigues por ella. Que la cuides como su hermanito, niñito Jesús, ayúdala la acompáñala, te encargo, en esto momento, que es la voluntad del espíritu, y el gran poder, y la voluntar del padre. En el nombre del padre, del hijo del espíritu santo.

Espíritu de, (person's name), ven a ella\el . . . (This phrase is repeated three times.)

Prayer for liberation of the soul (when weighed down by a problem, health, finances, or upon someone's death:

En el nombre de amadísima precensia: Yo soy, mi Cristo interno o mi verda·divina.

Yo invoco la Ley del Perdón y la llama violeta transmutadota para todos mis errores, que voluntaria o involuntariamente haya cometido, por el mal uso de la energía usada por mi en contra del reinó elemental, vegetal, animal, humano, y divino.

Por la soberbia, envidia, odio, celos, de sagrados, malas voluntades maledicencias, mentiras, venganzas, ira, gula, y enemigos mi existencia.

Yo soy el perdón a mi mismo, y perdono al los demás. Y comienzo de Nuevo

Gracias, Padre por oírme y liberarme.

Rays of light for meditation: a person is to envision him\herself surrounded by the particular ray of color for that day as he\she meditates. The patron divinity (-ies) for that day are included:

Monday: golden, divine understanding. Dedicated to Confucius
Tuesday: Rose, divine love, Pablo de Tarsas, lady Rowena; Archangel
            Chamuel
Wednesday: White, alleviation of a particular problem; Dedicated to the
            Archangel Gabriel, Serapis Bey
Thursday: Green, truth health, money; Dedicated to maestro Hilarion,
            Virgen Maria, Archangel Raphael.
Friday: Orange, healthy mind and for laziness. Dedicated to the
            maestro Jesus y Lady Nada
Saturday: Violet. healing light, transformation from a negative to a
            positive, pessimism to optimism. Dedicated to the teacher
            St. Germain
Sunday: light blue, for the government, lawyers, officials. Dedicated
            to the maestro Archangel Michael

Jo Ann and Lizzie in *barrida* rituals:

The Apostle's Creed:

> I believe in God the Father, almighty,
> creator of heaven and earth.
> I believe in Jesus Christ, his only son, our Lord
> born of the Virgin Mary.

He suffered under Pontius Pilate, was crucified,
died and was buried.
On the third day he rose again.
He ascended into heaven,
and is seated at the right hand of the Father.
He will come again to judge the living and the dead.
I believe in the Holy Spirit,
the holy Catholic Church,
the communion of saints,
the forgiveness of sins,
the resurrection of the body,
and the life everlasting. Amen.

Morning prayer on days of healing:

The shield of God protect us on this daily adventure, from evil, from witchcraft.

We ask for the Archangel Michael to battle unseen forces on our behalf so that we can help people find their spirituality, and help us to give them hope, so they do not have to suffer in this world; that they leave their tears and anxieties at our door, so that they can be whole with their families again.

Spiritual house cleansing:

Use equal parts of apple cider vinegar and holy water in a spray bottle. Going from room to room spray (in the sign of a cross) the corners of each room. As you do so, recite:

Lord's prayer

Our father who art in heaven hallowed be thy name
thy kingdom come, thy will be done on earth as it is in heaven.
Give us this day our daily bread and forgive us our trespasses
as we forgive those who trespassed against us
and lead us not into temptation but deliver us from evil. Amen.

Afterwards, sprinkle salt around the outside perimeter of your house.

NOTES

Introduction

1. Smith, *Decolonizing Methodologies: Research and Indigenous People*, 10.
2. Paredes, *Folklore and Culture on the Texas-Mexican Border*; John O. West, *Mexican-American Folklore*.

Chapter 1

1. A Tejano or Tejana is a person of Mexican descent born in Texas. The "j" is pronounced as an "h" sound as in the word "have."
2. Flores, *Remembering the Alamo: Memory, Modernity, and the Master Symbol*, 51.
3. Rodriguez, *San Antonio Express-News*.

Chapter 2

1. Cabeza de Vaca, "More Cures," 216.
2. Torres, "Curanderos and Shamans in the Southwest."
3. Martinez, *Border People*; Anzaldúa, 1987; Limón, "*Representation, Ethnicity, and the Precursory Ethnography.*"
4. Alvarez, "The Mexican-U.S. Border: The Making of an Anthropology of the Borderlands," 447–70.
5. For a discussion and references on class structure and hierarchy, see Vigil, "Colonial Institutions."
6. de la Casas, *In Defense of the Indians*, 12.
7. Ibid., 362.
8. Montejano, *Anglos and Mexicans in the Making of Texas, 1836–1968*, 83.
9. Madsen, *The Mexican-Americans of South Texas*.
10. Martin, *Flexible Bodies*, 4.

11. W. Madsen; Trotter and Chavira, *Curanderismo*; Ortiz de Montellano, *Aztec Medicine, Health, and Nutrition.*

12. Ford, *The Nature and Status of Ethnobotany*, 44.

Chapter 3

1. Etic refers to a cultural insider's perspective; emic is the understanding given for a cultural behavior or belief by an outside observer. For a varied discussion on emic/etic perspective by a native anthropologist please see Linda T. Smith, *Decolonizing Methodologies: Research and Indigenous Peoples.* Aside from the writers discussed in this chapter, Olga Najera Ramirez and Russell Bernard (*Research Methods in Anthropology: Qualitative and Quantitative Approaches.* Walnut Creek, Cal.: Alta Mira Press, 1995) might prove useful in this discussion.

2. Narayan, "How Native is a 'Native' Anthropologist?" 23.

3. Flores, *Remembering the Alamo: Memory, Modernity, and the Master Symbol*, xiii.

4. Ibid., xiv.

5. Macklin, "All the Good and Bad in This World," 127, 154. Límon, *Dancing With the Devil*, 202.

6. Límon, *Dancing With the Devil*, 203.

7. Tafolla. "Medicine Poem" in *Curandera*, 37.

8. Morales, *Medicine Stories: History, Culture and the Politics of Integrity*, 26–38.

9. There is a history in anthropology of a researcher becoming a practitioner of the tradition they are studying. Zora Neal Hurston, the folklorist, became a vodou practitioner during her fieldwork among African Americans in Florida during the late 1920s; see *Mules and Men.* Frank Hamilton Cushing joined the Priesthood of the Bow during his work with the Zuni in the 1880s; see *Cushing at Zuni: Correspondence and Journals.* Karen McCarthy Brown was initiated into vodou religion by a vodou priestess, Alourdes, during her fieldwork in Brooklyn; see *Mama Lola: A Vodou Priestess in Brooklyn.*

10. Leyva, "There is great good in returning," 5.

11. Historian as Curandera, Aurora Levin Morales, "Medicine Stories," 23.

12. Ibid.

13. Brave Heart, "The historical trauma response among natives and its relationship with substance abuse: a Lakota illustration," 7–13. Dr. Brave Heart is an associate professor at Columbia University School of Social Work. Dr. Brave Heart developed the concept of historical trauma along with theory and intervention practices for dealing with its effects among Native Americans.

14. Moraga and Anzaldúa, *This Bridge Called My Back: Writings by Radical Women of Color*, 23.

15. Narayan, 37.

16. Behar, *The Vulnerable Observer: Anthropology that breaks your heart*, 174.

17. Narayan, 37.

18. Dominguez, "For a Politics of Love and Rescue," 361–93.

19. Smith, 14–16.

20. Guillermo Bonfil Batalla, *Mexico Profundo: Reclaiming a Civilization* (Austin: University of Texas Press, 1996), xvi. Bonfil Batalla's writings reflect an idea of building a society that values contributions from culturally diverse peoples as equal in all manners. *Indios* are part of this Mexico, and he writes of the history of Mexico as one where the *Indio* is constantly under the threat of erasure. Before Mexico can move forward, he argues, its treatment of the indigenous must be confronted and remedied.

21. For a discussion on violence and Chicano\as see Eden Torre, *Chicana without Apology: The New Chicana Cultural Studies* (New York: Routledge, 2003).

22. Saldívar, 6.

23. Ibid., 6.

24. Romero, "Life as a Maid's Daughter: An Exploration of the Everyday Boundaries of Race, Class, and Gender."

25. Ibid, 194–209.

26. Ochs and Capps, "Narrating the Self," 19–43.

27. Romero, 204.

28. Riessman, "Introduction: Locating Narratives and Theoretical Context," 8.

29. W. Madsen in Kiev, *Magic, Faith, and Healing*, 420–40.

30. Hart, *New Voices in the Nation: Women and the Greek Resistance 1941–1964.*

31. Mayers, "Use of Medicine by Elderly Mexican-American Women," 283–95; Edgerton, "Curanderismo in the Metropolis: The Diminished Role of folk Psychiatry Among Los Angeles Mexican-Americans," 124–34; Graham, "The Role of Curanderismo in the Mexican-American Folk Medicine System in West Texas," 180.

Chapter 4

1. Trotter and Chavira, 7.

2. Gaines, *Ethnopsychiatry: The Cultural Construction of Professional and Folk Psychiatries*, 413; Mayers, 285; Gaines, 411.

3. R. Mayers; Rivera, "AIDS and Mexican Folk Medicine," 3–7; Urdaneta and others, "Mexican-American Perceptions of Severe Mental Illness;" Applewhite, "Curanderismo: Demystifying the Health Beliefs and Practices of Mexican-American Women," 247–53.

4. Trotter and Chavira, 61–64.

5. Trotter and Chavira, 64.

6. de Waal Malefijt, "Religious Healing," Chapter 10.

7. Batalla, 17, 75.

8. Menchaca, Martha. "Chicano Indianism: An Historical Account of Racial Repression in the United States," 583–603.

9. Avila, "Dispelling the Sombras, *Grito mi nombre con rayos de luz*," 238.

10. Redfield, "Folk Culture of the Yucatan."

11. Norman Taylor in Omer Stewart's *Peyote Religion*, 20.

12. For a discussion on Quinceañeras see Karen Mary Dávalos, "*La Quince-añera*: Making Gender and Ethnic Identities," 101–27. Also see Norma E. Cantú, "La Quinceañera: Towards an Analysis of a Life Cycle Ritual," in *Southern Folklore* 56, No. 1 (1999): 73–101.

13. Espín, "Popular Catholicism Among Latinos," 308–59.

14. C. Perez-Bustamante, *Don Antonio de Mendoza, primer virrey de la Nueva España* (Santiago de Compostela, 1928), 161; de la Mota Padilla, "Historia de la Conquista de la Provincia de la Nueva Galicia (Mexico 1870)," chapter 26; Bruel, "Les foctions mentales dans les sociétés inférieures (Paris 1931)," 74–76; Ricard, *Spiritual Conquest of Mexico*, 266.

15. Ricard, 267.

16. Ibid., 267.

17. Ibid., 268.

18. Bell, *Ritual Perspectives and Dimensions*, 111.

19. Foster, "Relationships Between Spanish and Spanish-American Folk Medicine," 28; Claudia Madsen, "A Study of Change in Mexican Folk Medicine," 25: 97; William Madsen, 70.

20. Trotter and Chavira, 29.

21. W. Madsen, *La Raza*, Chapter 2.

22. Ibid., 16.

23. Trotter and Chavira, 29–30.

24. Ross, "Lama Govinda" in *Buddhism: Way of Life & Thought*, 119.

Chapter 5

1. Trotter and Chavira, 81.

2. What I found disturbing in ethnographic accounts, e.g. Madsen, is the tendency to take literally the descriptions of their consultants as to "little animals" (germs) in the body as opposed to their thinking in terms of metaphor.

3. Trotter and Chavira, 114–16.

4. Ibid., 64.

5. Ibid., 105.

6. Ibid., 81.

7. Alan Dundes, folklorist from University of California at Berkeley, edited a volume on evil eye and its cross-cultural presence throughout Europe, Asia, and the Mediterranean: please see *The Evil Eye: A Casebook* (Madison: University of Wisconsin press).

8. Kleinman, *Patients and Healers in the Context of Culture: An Exploration of the Borderland Between Anthropology, Medicine, and Psychiatry*.

9. Csordas, "The Affliction of Martin: Religious, Clinical, and Phenomenological Meaning in a case of Demonic Oppression," 154.

10. Des Jarlais, "Struggling Along," 70.

11. D. E. Alegria, "El Hospital Invisible: A Study of Curanderismo," 1354–67.

12. R. Mayers; M. Urdaneta; Trotter, "Contrasting Models of the Healer's Role: South Texas Case Examples," 315–17.

13. For a discussion of Coatlique, see Anzaldúa's *Borderlands/la Frontera* and *Interviews/Entrevistas*. The way I use Coatique, Nepantla, and Nahutl came from *Interviews/Entrevistas*, 224–26.

14. These quotes are from the healing ceremony Golondrina performed on me after the car wreck discussed earlier.

15. Haraway, *Simians, Cyborgs, and Women*, 208.

16. Martin, 14, 15.

17. Ibid., 15.

18. Trotter and Chavira, 51.

19. Trotter and Chavira, 61.

20. For an anthropological explanation on the system of *compadrazgo*, see Robert Lavenda and Emily Schultz, *Core Concepts in Cultural Anthropology* (McGraw-Hill, 2007), 101. In South Texas among Mexican Americans the system of *compadrazgo* is based less on a patronage system than what is practiced in most of Latin America. Its focus is acknowledging systems of support between individuals whether those are based on a religious precept or on close friendships.

Chapter 6

1. Heinrich, "Medicinal Plants in Mexico: Healer's Consensus and Cultural Importance," 1859–71; Ortiz de Montellano, *Aztec Medicine, Health, and Nutrition*; Stepp, "Mountain Ethnobiology and Development in Highland Chiapas, Mexico: Lessons in Biodiversity and Health," 219.

2. Kay, *Healing with Plants in the American and Mexican West*; Ford, *Las Yerbas de la Gente: A Study of Hispano-American Medicinal Plants*.

3. Carlson and Jones, "Some Notes on Uses of Plants by the Comanche Indian"; Cushing, "Zuni Breadstuff," 1–673.

4. Kay. *Healing with Plants in the American and Mexican West*; Nina Etkin, *Eating on the Wild Side: The Pharmacologic, Ecologic, and Social Implications of Using Noncultigens* (Tucson: University of Arizona Press, 1994); Gary Nabhan, *The Desert Smells Like Rain: A Naturalist in Papago Indian Country* (San Francisco: North Point Press, 1982).

5. Moore, 14.

6. Ibid.

Chapter 7

1. Montejano, *Anglos and Mexicans and the Making of Texas, 1836–1986*; Arnoldo De Leon, *Mexican Americans in Texas*, (Arlington Heights, Illinois: Harlan Davidson, 1993).

2. For example, *Curandersimo* by Trotter and Chavira is based on data collected under *Proyecto Comprender* (Regional Medical Program of Texas Grant 75–108G).

3. Manuel, *Spanish-Speaking Children of the Southwest*, 35; Moore and Cuellar, 130. Both works use Florence R. Kluckhohn's work on New Mexico Hispanics, *Variations in Value Orientation* (Evanston, Illinois: Row, Peterson and Co., 1961).

4. William Madsen's, Claudia Madsen's, and Ari Kiev's writings present stereotypical views of Mexicans and Mexican Americans in keeping with popular viewpoints of the day.

5. Anzaldúa, *Borderlands, La Frontera*, 99.

6. Ibid., 100.

7. Saldívar-Hull, *Feminism on the Border*, 29–34. Saldívar-Hull discusses the antecedents to Chicana feminism, its development and self-definition in part as a reaction to the male centered history and politics of the Chicano Movement.

8. Ibid., 63–67.

9. Also see Avila's work named earlier in the text and Yolanda Broyles-Gonzalez's "Indianizing Catholicism: Chicana/India/Mexicana Indigenous Spiritual Practices in Our Image" in *Chicana Traditions: Continuity and Change*," eds. Norma E. Cantú and Olga Nájera-Ramírez (Chicago: University of Illinois Press, 2002), 117.

10. de la Portilla, E. (1995), "Comanche and Mexican-American Curers: A regional approach to folk medicine," in *Touchstone*, The Texas State Historical Association: U.S.A., vol. XIV: 70–90.

11. Rodriguez, *Our Lady of Guadalupe: Faith and Empowerment among Mexican American Women*, xix.

12. Virgilio P. Elizondo, *The Future is Mestizo: Life Where Cultures Meet* (University Press of Colorado, 2000).

13. Gonzales, "Pot of Tears."

14. *La llorona* in folklore was a woman who drowned her children so that her lover (who didn't want them) would marry her. He then refused her on the grounds that she was a murderess. She is damned to wander the earth until she recovers *los niños*. She wails through the night, searching for her children and crying for her sin. The story has been rewritten through the ages to reflect regional geography or historical events. Marina, Cortez's Indian mistress, in the past was identified as *la llorona* because she is thought to have betrayed her people. There is indication that the motif of *la llorona* came with the Spanish, originally as a cautionary tale.

15. Patrisia Gonzales in conversation, April 6, 2002.

16. Leyva, "There Is Great Good in Returning." The initial quote, "I am who I am because I have been there . . ." is from Momaday, "Revisiting Sacred Ground," 118.

17. Eduardo Duran and Bonnie Duran, *Native American Postcolonial Psychology*.

18. Gonzales, "Trauma, Love, & History."

19. Edén Torres, *Chicana without Apology*.

20. In conversation, April 2002.

BIBLIOGRAPHY

Alcorn, Janis B. *Huastec Mayan Ethnobotany.* Austin: University of Texas Press, 1984.

Alegria, D. E. Guerra, M. Cervando, and G. G. Meyer. 1977. "El Hospital Invisible: A Study of Curanderismo." *Archives of General Psychiatry* 34: 1354–67.

Alvarez, Robert R. 1995. "The Mexican-US Border: The Making of an Anthropology of the Borderlands." *Annual Review of Anthropology. Annual Reviews Inc.* 24: 447–470.

Anaya, Rudolfo A. *Bless Me, Ultima.* Berkeley: TQS Publications, 1994.

Anderson, Edgar. *Plants, Man and Life.* Berkeley: University of California Press, 1952.

Anzaldúa, Gloria. *Borderlands: La frontera.* San Francisco: Spinsters/Aunt Lute, 1987.

———. *Interviews/Entrevistas.* Edited by Ana Louise Keating. New York: Routledge, 2000.

Applewhite, Steven L. 1995. "Curanderismo: Demystifying the Health Beliefs and Practices of Elderly Mexican-American Women." *Health & Social Work* 20: 247–553.

Avila, Inés Hernández. "Dispelling the Sombras, Grito Mi Nombre con Rayos de Luz. *Telling to Live: Latina Feminist Testimonios by the Latina Feminist Group.* Durham: Duke University Press, 2001.

Bannon, John F. *Bolton and the Spanish Borderlands.* Norman: University of Oklahoma Press, 1968.

Behar, Ruth. *Translated Woman: Crossing the Border with Esperanza's Story.* Boston: Beacon Press, 1993.

———. *The Vulnerable Observer: Anthropology that Breaks your Heart.* Boston: Beacon Press, 1996.

Bell, Catherine. *Ritual Perspectives and Dimensions.* New York: Oxford University Press, 1997.

Berlandier, Jean Louis. *The Indians of Texas in 1830.* Edited by J. C. Ewers. Washington D.C.: Smithsonian Institution Press, 1969.

Brave Heart, M. Y. 2003. "The historical trauma response among natives and its relationship with substance abuse: a Lakota illustration." *Journal of Psychoactive Drugs*, 35(1): 7–13.

Brown, Karen McCarthy. *Mama Lola: A Vodou Priestess in Brooklyn*. Berkeley: University of California Press, 1991.

Bruel, Lucien Levy. "Les foctions mentales dans les societes infetieures." In Robert Ricard's *Spiritual Conquest of Mexico*. Berkeley: University of California Press, 1966.

Bustamante, C. Perez. 1928. "Don Antoniode Mendoza, primer virrey de la Nueva Espana (Santiago de Compostela)" in Robert Ricard's *Spiritual Conquest of Mexico*, Berkeley: University of California Press, 1966.

Butler, Judith. *Bodies That Matter*. New York: Routledge, 1993.

Cabeza de Vaca, Alvar Nuñez. "More Cures." *Adventures in the Unknown Interior of America*. Translated by Cyclone Covey. New York: Crowell-Collier Publishing Company, 1961.

Carlson, Gustov and Volney Jones. 1940. *Some Notes on Uses of Plants by the Comanche Indians*. Reprinted from Papers of the Michigan Academy of Science, Arts, and Letters, Vol. XXV.

Cantú, Norma, and Olga Nájera-Ramírez, eds. *Chicana Traditions: Continuity and Change*. Chicago: University of Illinois Press, 2002.

Csordas, Thomas J. "The Affliction of Martin: Religious, Clinical, and Phenomenological Meaning in a case of Demonic Oppression." *Ethnopsychiatry: The Cultural Construction of Professional and Folk Psychiatries*. Edited by Atwood Gaines. Albany: University of New York Press, 1992.

Cushing, Frank. 1920. "Zuni Breadstuff." *Indian Notes and Monographs* 8: 1–673.

de la Casas, Bartholomé. *In Defense of the Indians*. Translated by Stafford Poole. DeKalb: Northern Illinois Press, 1992.

de la Mota Padilla, Matias. "Historia de la Conquista de la Provincia de la Nueva Galicia." *Spiritual Conquest of Mexico*. Edited by Robert Ricard. Berkley: University of California Press, 1966.

de la Portilla, Elizabeth. 1995. "Comanche and Mexican-American Curers: A Regional Approach to Folk Medicine." *Touchstone*. The Texas State Historical Association Vol. XIV: 70–90.

de Waal Malefijt, Annamarie. *Religion and Culture: An Introduction to Anthropology Healing*. Prospect Heights, Ill.: Waveland Press, 1989.

Des Jarlais, Robert. "Struggling Along." *Things As They Are: New Direction in Phenomenological Anthropology*. Edited by R. Jackson. Bloomington: Indiana Press, 1996.

Dominquez, Virginia. 2000. "For a Politics of Love and Rescue." *Cultural Anthropology* 15(3): 361–93.

Duran, Eduardo, and Bonnie Duran. *Native American Postcolonial Psychology*. Albany State: University of New York Press, 1995.

Edgerton, Robert, and others. 1970. "Curanderismo in the Metropolis: The Diminished Role of Folk Psychiatry Among Los Angeles Mexican-Americans." *American Journal of Psychotherapy* 24: 124–34.

Espín, Orlando. "Popular Catholicism Among Latinos." *Hispanic Catholic Culture in the U.S.* J. P. Dolan and Allan Figueroa Deck, S.J., editors. Notre Dame: University of Notre Dame Press, 1997.

Etkin, Nina L., editor. *Plants in Medicine and Diet.* Bedford Hills, NY: Redgrave Publishing Co., 1986.

Flores, Richard R. *Remembering the Alamo: Memory, Modernity, and the Master Symbol.* Austin: University of Texas Press, 2002.

Ford, Karen C. *Las Yerbas de la Gente: A Study of Hispano-American Medicinal Plants.* Ann Arbor: University of Michigan Press, 1975.

Ford, Richard I., editor. *The Nature and Status of Ethnobotany.* Anthropological Papers, Museum of Anthropology No. 67. Ann Arbor: University of Michigan, 1994.

Foster, George. 1953. "Relationships Between Spanish and Spanish-American Folk Medicine." *Journal of Amercian Folklore* 66: 202–203.

Furst, Peter. *Hallucinogens and Culture.* Novato, California: Chandler and Sharp, 1982.

Gaines, Atwood, editor. *Ethnopsychiatry: The Cultural Construction of Professional and Folk Psychiatries.* Albany: University of New York Press, 1992.

Graham, J. S. "The Role of Curanderismo in the Mexican-American Folk Medicine System in West Texas. *American Folk Medicine: A Symposium.* Edited by W. D. Hand. Berkeley: University of California Press, 1976.

Gonzales, Patrisia. "Pot of Tears." *Column of the Americas,* March, 2002. Copyright Patrisia Gonzales and Roberto Rodriguez.

———. "Trauma, Love, & History." *Column of the Americas,* February 6, 2006.

Haraway, Donna. *Simians, Cyborgs, and Women.* New York: Routledge, 1991.

Hart, Janet. *New Voices in the Nation: Women and the Greek Resistance 1941–1964.* Ithaca: Cornell University Press, 1996.

Heinrich, Michael, and others. 1998. "Medicinal Plants in Mexico: Healer's Consensus and Cultural Importance." *Social Science and Medicine* 47(11): 1859–71.

Hurston, Zora Neale. *Mules and Men.* New York: Harper Perennial Modern Classics, 2008.

Jackson, Michael, editor. *Things As They Are: New Direction in Phenomenological Anthropology.* Bloomington: Indiana Press, 1996.

Kay, Margarita A. *Healing with Plants in the American and Mexican West.* Tucson: University of Arizona Press, 1996.

Kennedy, Jesse, editor. *Cushing at Zuni: Correspondence and Journals.* Albuquerque: University of New Mexico Press, 1990.

Kiev, Ari. *Magic, Faith, and Healing.* New York: Free Press, 1964.

Kleinman, Arthur. *Patients and Healers in the Context of Culture: An Exploration of the Borderland Between Anthropology, Medicine, and Psychiatry.* Berkeley: University of California Press, 1980.

Latina Feminist Group. *Telling to Live: Latina Feminist Testimonios.* Durham: Duke University Press, 2001.

Leyva, Yolanda Chavez . "There is Great Good in Returning: A Testimonio from the Borderlands." *Frontiers: A Journal of Women's Studies.* (forthcoming).

Límon, José. "Representation, Ethnicity, and the Precursory Ethnography." *Recapturing Anthropology.* Edited by Richard Fox. Santa Fe: School for Advanced Research Press, 1991.

————. *Dancing with the Devil.* Madison: University of Wisconsin Press, 1994.

Macklin, June. "'All the Good and Bad in This World': Women, Traditional Medicine, and Mexican American Culture." *Twice a Minority: Mexican American Women.* Edited by Margarita Melville. St. Louis: C.V. Mosby, 1980.

Madsen, Claudia. 1968. "A Study of Change in Mexican Folk Medicine." *Middle America Research Institution* 25: 89–138.

Madsen, William. *The Mexican-Americans of South Texas.* New York: Holt, Rhinehart and Winston, Inc., 1964.

Martin, Emily. *Flexible Bodies.* Boston: Beacon Press, 1994.

Martinez, Oscar J. *Border People.* Tucson: University of Arizona Press, 1994.

Manuel, Herschal T. *Spanish-Speaking Children of the Southwest.* Austin: University of Texas Press, 1965.

Mayers, Raymond S. 1989. "Use of Medicine by Elderly Mexican-American Women." *Journal of Drug Issues* 19(2): 283–95.

Menchaca, Martha. 1993. "Chicano Indianism: A Historical Account of Racial Repression in the United States." *American Ethnologist* 20(3): 583–603.

Momaday, N. Scott. "Revisiting Sacred Ground." *The Man Made of Words.* New York: St. Martin's Press, 1997.

Montejano, David. *Anglos and Mexicans in the Making of Texas, 1836–1936.* Austin: University of Texas Press, 1987.

Moraga, Cherrie, and Gloria Anzaldúa, editors. *This Bridge Called My Back: Writings by Radical Women of Color.* New York: Kitchen Table: Women of Color Press, 1983.

Morales, Aurora Levins. *Medicine Stories: History, Culture and the Politics of Integrity.* Cambridge, MA: South End Press, 1998.

Moore, Joan, and Alfredo Cuellar. *Mexican Americans.* Englewood Cliffs, N.J.: Prentice-Hall, 1970.

Moore, Michael. *Los Remedios: Traditional Herbal Remedies of the Southwest.* Santa Fe: Red Crane Books, 1990.

Narayan, Kirin. "How Native is a 'Native' Anthropologist?" *Situated Lives: Gender and Culture in Everyday Life.* Edited by L. Lamphere, H. Ragone, and Patricia Zavella. New York: Routledge Press, 1997.

Ochs, Elinor, and Lisa Capps. 1996. "Narrating the Self." *Annual Review of Anthropology* 5: 19–43.

Ortiz de Montellano, Bernardo. *Aztec Medicine, Health, and Nutrition.* New Brunswick: Rutgers University Press, 1990.

Paredes, Américo. *Folklore and Culture on the Texas-Mexico Border.* Edited by Richard Bauman CMAS. Austin: University of Texas Press, 1993.

Redfield, Robert. "Folk Culture of the Yucatan." *Anthropology of Folk Religion*, edited by Charles Leslie. New York: Random House, 1960.

Ricard, Robert. *Spiritual Conquest of Mexico*. Berkeley: University of California Press, 1966.

Riessman, Catherine K. "Introduction: Locating Narratives and Theoretical Contexts." *Narrative Analysis: Qualitative Research Methods Series*. Thousand Oaks: Sage, 1993.

Rivera, George Jr. October 1990. "AIDS and Mexican Folk Medicine." *Sociology and Social Research* 75: 3–7.

Rodriguez, Ihosvani. *San Antonio Express-News*, September 2000.

Rodriguez, Jeanette. *Our Lady of Guadalupe: Faith, and Empowerment among Mexican American Women*. Austin: University of Texas Press, 1994.

Romero, Mary. "Life As a Maid's Daughter: An Exploration of the Everyday Boundaries of Race, Class, and Gender." *Challenging Fronteras: Structuring Latina and Latino Lives in the U.S.* New York: Routledge, 1997.

Rubel, Arthur J. 1978. "Difficulties of Presenting Complaints to Physicians: Susto as an Example." *Modern Medicine and Medical Anthropology in the United States-Mexico border Population*. Edited by Boris Velimirovic. Washington D.C.: Pan American Health Organization. Scientific Publication No. 359.

Saldívar, Ramon. *Chicano Narrative: The Dialectics of Difference*. Madison: University of Wisconsin Press, 1990.

Saldívar-Hull, Sonia. *Feminism on the Border: Chicana Gender Politics and Literature*. Berkeley: University of California Press, 2000.

Smith, Linda Tuhiwai. *Decolonizing Methodologies: Research and Indigenous People*. Dunedin, New Zealand: Zed Books, 2002.

Stewart, Omer. *Peyote Religion*. Norman: University of Oklahoma Press, 1987.

Stepp, J. R. August 2000. "Mountain Ethnobiology and Development in Highland Chiapas, Mexico: Lessons in Biodiversity and Health." *Mountain Research and Development* 20: 219.

Tafolla, Carmen. *Curandera*. Santa Monica, California: Santa Monica College Press, 1992.

Torres, Edén. *Chicana without Apology: The New Chicana Cultural Studies*. New York: Routledge, 2003.

Torres, Eliseo. "Curanderos and Shamans in the Southwest," University of New Mexico in Albuquerque, New Mexico, 1996. http://www.hartford-hwp.com/archives/41/251.html.

Trotter, Robert, 1982. "Contrasting Models of the Healer's Role: South Texas Case Examples." *Hispanic Journal of Behavioral Sciences* 4: 315–17.

Trotter, Robert. and Joan Chavira. *Curanderismo*. Athens: University of Georgia Press, 1981.

Urdaneta, Mary, Delia Huron-Saldaña, and Anne Winkler. 1995. "Mexican-American Perceptions of Severe Mental Illness." *Human Organization* 54: 1.

Vigil, Ralph. "Colonial Institutions." *Borderlands Sourcebook*. Edited by Ellwyn R.

Stoddard, Richard L. Nostrand, and Jonathon P. West. Norman: University of Oklahoma Press, 1983.

Vogel, Virgil. *American Indian Medicine.* Norman: University of Oklahoma Press, 1970.

West, John O. *Mexican-American Folklore.* Little Rock: August House, 1989.

Wilson Ross, Nancy. *Buddhism: Way of Life and Thought.* New York: Alfred Knopf, 1980.

INDEX

Spaniards, 59
Spanish, 21–22, 32, 43–44, 54–55, 60, 62, 105
Spanish American, 62
Spanish Mexican, 16
Stern, Alexandera Minna, 112
stratification, 16
stratified, 21
substitution;
    Altamisa, 100
    Altamisa Mexicana, 100
    wormwood, 100
superbueno, 98
susto (magical fright), 30, 80
sweet bread, 13

taco, papa con egg, 10
Tafolla, Carmen, 35–36, 107
tantric mysticism, 63
taxonomy, 100
Tejanos, 11
Texans, 22
Texas, 7, 34;
    Austin, 9–11
    Central, 8
    Corpus Christi, 14, 101, 109
    Dallas, 10
    East, 8
    far west, 8
    Gulf coast, 14
    Hill Country, 9, 11
    Houston, 10–11
    Jasper, 9
    Laredo, 109
    San Antonio, 9–16, 21, 23–26, 29, 38,
        44–45, 54, 57, 60, 62, 69, 77, 94, 98,
        111, 115, 118
    South, 8, 9, 25, 34, 97, 116
    Southwest, 4
Texas Rangers, 48

Texas Revolution, 8, 22
theaters;
    Alameda, 15
    Aztec, 15
    Majestic, 15
    Nacional, 15
theological studies, 34
Third World, 21
Tío Jesse, 14
Tonatzin at Tepeyac, 58
Torres, Eden, 112
Torres, Eliseo, 20
trios, 12, 83
triumphalist literature, 22
Trotter, Robert, 52, 62–63, 72–74, 99

United States, 10, 25, 27, 32, 44, 47, 85, 96
University of Auckland, New Zealand, 3
University of Michigan, 117
University of Texas Health Science Center,
    108
University of Wisconsin, 2
U.S.–Mexico borderland, 21

Vangie, 112–113
Van Gogh, 15
vato locos, 105
Vietnamese, 11
Virgen, 57
Virgen de Guadalupe, 58, 60, 104, 107
Virgilio, Don, 55, 70, 73, 76
vodou, 60

West, John O., 4
white, 105
working-class, 3, 4, 14, 23

yerberias, 68
Ytuarte, Esperanza, 15